THE EXPERTS SPEAK

> THE TESTIMONY OF:
> J. Gordon Melton
> John A. Saliba
> Eugene Van Ness Goetchius
> Rodney Stark
> H. Newton Malony
> Edwin S. Gaustad

CONCERNING WITNESS LEE AND THE LOCAL CHURCHES

Living Stream Ministry
Anaheim, California

© 1995 Living Stream Ministry

First Edition, 4,500 copies. November 1995.

ISBN 0-87083-918-7

Published by

Living Stream Ministry
1853 W. Ball Road, Anaheim, CA 92804 U.S.A.
P. O. Box 2121, Anaheim, CA 92814 U.S.A.

Printed in the United States of America

CONTENTS

Chapter		Page
	Preface	5
	Meet the Experts	7
1	Introduction	11
2	The Testimony of John Gordon Melton, Ph.D.	19
3	The Testimony of John Albert Saliba, Ph.D.	85
4	The Testimony of Eugene Van Ness Goetchius, Ph.D, Th.D.	109
5	The Testimony of Rodney Stark, Ph.D.	129
6	The Testimony of H. Newton Malony, Ph.D.	147
7	The Testimony of Edwin S. Gaustad, Ph.D.	197
	Appendix	201
	Index	203

PREFACE

The Experts Speak is the testimony of five expert witnesses who testified on behalf of Witness Lee and the local churches in Alameda County Superior Court on May 28 and 31, 1985. The final expert, Dr. Edwin S. Gaustad, was not asked to testify at the trial but wrote the included article entitled, "Libel and the First Amendment." (For a detailed background of the court case, see the introduction.)

The testimony of these experts, as contained in this book, remains the same as that of the public court transcripts; however, minor changes were made to complete thoughts and sentences based on a comparison of the transcripts with the audio tapes of the trial. The experts have reviewed the edited transcripts presented in this book, and any corrections that they felt were necessary are included.

The book takes this basic form: The questions asked by the attorney representing the local churches, Mr. Charles Morgan, are followed by the answers given by each of the experts. Judge Leon Seyranian takes an active role in the interchange. The questions and comments by the attorney and the judge are italicized to distinguish them from the testimony of the experts. Whenever the judge is addressed or speaks, the speaker's name has been indented. The style is meant to reflect the format of the original court record.

Throughout the trial, references are made to four versions of *The God-Men:* (1) *The God-Men I,* or *The God-Men: Witness Lee and the Local Church* (80 pages); (2) the Duddy manuscript; (3) the German edition, or *Die Sonderlehre des Witness Lee und seiner Ortsgemeinde;* and (4) *The God-Men II,* or *The God-Men: An Inquiry into Witness Lee and the Local Church* (156 pages).

MEET THE EXPERTS

JOHN GORDON MELTON, Ph.D.

Dr. Melton is the Director of the Institute for the Study of American Religion and Visiting Scholar at the University of California at Santa Barbara. The Institute is the largest research facility in the United States engaged in scholarly research on the many different religious groups in North America. He is the author of over twelve books on American religious groups including the *Encyclopedia of American Religions* (3 vols.), the standard reference work in its field. Among his other books are: *The Dictionary of Religious Bodies in the United States*; *The Cult Experience; The Old Catholic Sourcebook; Why Cults Succeed When Churches Fail; The Biographical Dictionary of Sect and Cult Leaders;* the *Encyclopedia Handbook of the Cults*; *American Religious Creeds;* and *the Encyclopedic Handbook of Cults in America.*

Dr. Melton is an ordained minister in the United Methodist Church and a member of its Northern Illinois Conference. He has a Ph.D. in the History and Literature of Religion from Northwestern University (1975) and a Master of Divinity in Church History from Garret Evangelical Theological Seminary (1968). Versed in Methodist history, he served on the editorial board and wrote a number of articles for the *Encyclopedia of World Methodism.*

JOHN ALBERT SALIBA, Ph.D.

Father Saliba is a Catholic priest and a member of the Jesuit order. He is a professor in the Department of Religious Studies at the University of Detroit, specializing in the anthropology of religion. He has written four books including: *'Homo Religious' in Mircea Eliade: An Anthropological Evaluation*, *Psychiatry and the Cults: An Annotated Bibliography;* and *Social Science and the Cults: An Annotated Bibliography.* He received his Ph.D. from the Department of Religion of the Catholic University in Washington.

EUGENE VAN NESS GOETCHIUS, Ph.D., Th.D.

Reverend Goetchius, now retired, was professor of Biblical Languages from 1963–1989, holding chairs simultaneously in the Episcopal Theological School and the Philadelphia Divinity School. He taught Greek and Hebrew and collaborated with colleagues from Harvard Divinity School and Weston School of Theology, in teaching introductory courses in New Testament interpretation and exegesis. He wrote a Greek grammar book, *The Language of the New Testament* with an accompanying workbook; *The Teaching of the Biblical Languages* and *The Gifts of God*. He received his Th.D. in New Testament Studies from Union Theological Seminary in New York in 1963 and his Ph.D. in Germanic Languages and Linguistics from the University of Virginia in 1949.

RODNEY STARK, Ph.D.

Dr. Stark is professor of Sociology and Comparative Religion at the University of Washington. He is renowned in the field of the sociology of religion with particular emphasis on religious movements. He is perhaps best known for being a co-author of the Lofland-Stark Model of Conversion, which the author of *The God-Men* invoked in an attempt to criticize the local church.

Dr. Stark received his Ph.D. in Sociology from the University of California at Berkeley. He has authored over a dozen books and numerous articles on the sociology of religion.

H. NEWTON MALONY, Ph.D.

Dr. Malony is the Senior Professor of Psychology in the Graduate School of Psychology at Fuller Theological Seminary and a practicing psychologist. Dr. Malony is a Fellow of the American Psychological Association, a Diplomate in Clinical Psychology of the American Board of Professional Psychology and received the Distinguished Member Award in 1987 from the Christian Association for Psychological Studies.

Dr. Malony has published over 30 books and has been a

contributing editor to seven professional journals. A few of his books include: *Current Perspectives in the Psychology of Religion; Conversion: Biblical and Psychological Perspectives; Religion and Mental Illness: A Directory of Programs Sponsored by Churches and Congregations*; *Psychology of Religion: Personalities, Problems, Possibilities;* and the *Handbook on Conversion.*

In addition to his Ph.D. in Psychology from George Peabody College of Vanderbilt University in 1964, Dr. Malony received a M.Div. from Yale Divinity School in 1955. He is an ordained minister of the United Methodist Church and a member of the Pacific and Southwest Annual Conference.

EDWIN S. GAUSTAD, Ph.D.

Dr. Gaustad is an Emeritus Professor of History from the University of California, Riverside. He has been a visiting professor at Baylor University, the University of Richmond, Princeton Theological Seminary, and Auburn University. In 1993 Dr. Gaustad received the Eminent Scholar in Religion award from Auburn University. He is the past President of the American Society of Church History.

Dr. Gaustad has published 12 books including: *Historical Atlas of Religion in America; A Religious History of America; Religious Issues in American History;* and was editor of *Documentary History of Religion in America* (2 vols.). He was the editor (with R.A. Spivey and R.F. Allen) of high school materials for teaching about religion in the Social Studies curriculum (all published by Addison-Wesley): *Religious Issues in American Culture; Religious Issues in Western Civilization;* and *Religious Issues in World Civilization.*

CHAPTER ONE

INTRODUCTION

The Experts Speak records the sworn testimony of the expert witnesses at the trial of *Lee v. Duddy, et al* in the Superior Court of California in May 1985. Six experts, representing diverse religious backgrounds, were asked to study the teachings and practices of Witness Lee and the local churches. The experts were also asked to study the charges and criticisms printed against the local churches in the book, *The God-Men,* published by Spiritual Counterfeits Project (SCP). Finally, five of these men were asked to present their conclusions under oath in the Superior Court of California. The sixth expert, Dr. Gaustad, did not testify at the trial, but his research was summarized in a paper that is reprinted in this book. This is their expert testimony concerning Witness Lee and the local churches.

The lawsuit was not over doctrinal differences, but libel, claiming *The God-Men* presented a false, malicious and damaging portrayal of Witness Lee and the local churches. Yet the many charges used by SCP to create the "cult" image were related to the churches' beliefs and practices. Their accusations were a mixture of theology, psychology, sociology, and "factual" events. Thus, the total misrepresentation of the book, including doctrine, had to be demonstrated. Since SCP had set itself up as the expert in judging the local churches, it was essential to obtain the testimony of some who were more qualified in the fields involved. For this reason, qualified experts in each area were sought out and asked to study the local churches and to evaluate the charges in *The God-Men.* The conclusions of truly qualified experts concerning both the local churches and their critics can be found in *The Experts Speak.*

Why did those in the local churches bring suit against other Christians? The first choice in resolving conflicts among Christians is, of course, not the law courts (1 Cor. 6). According to the admonition of Scripture, attempts should be made by Christian brothers to solve a problem by way of Christian fellowship (Matt. 18:15). Unfortunately, the attitude of SCP from the early 1970's was never that of brothers seeking truth or reconciliation with other Christians. Rather, from the first, their attitude was to judge, condemn, and destroy a "spiritual counterfeit" that they never really understood. SCP ignored repeated efforts by those in the churches to point out their error.

A manuscript was produced by SCP in 1976 that eventually became the first edition of *The God-Men*. Ultimately, another book came out of that one manuscript, Jack Sparks and others developing it into *The Mindbenders*. Jack Sparks had been an early leader among SCP. He was then in the process of breaking with SCP to join with other previous associates from a local church splinter group. Sparks provided a copy of the SCP manuscript to embittered members of the splinter group. That manuscript was developed into *The Mindbenders*.

Thus, two books were published in 1977, apparently from different sources, but actually cloned from one manuscript. They are so similar that they even reproduce the same typographical errors in the original manuscript. It is no wonder their arguments and conclusions are so similar. Strong protest was made against both books by members of the churches before their publication. Both were published, however, despite those protests.

As a result, these two books became extremely damaging to those in the local churches. At first, those in the local churches naively felt that no one would believe books that were so far from the truth. Yet because no protest to those books reached the public, people accepted their accusations as truth. The charges were republished in the media as fact again and again. Within a year the local churches were on everyone's "cult" list. Once the local churches were labeled a cult, the response was automatic. People reacted with suspicion, fear, contempt, and avoidance, and these reactions were beyond the power of reason to dispel. There was no way to get a public forum to correct the error. No bookstore wanted to carry the reply of a group branded as a "cult." The members of the local churches experienced and endured severe problems in their work; some lost their jobs. More emotionally wrenching were the problems in family relationships as frightened parents and friends tried to "rescue" loved ones. The outreach of the local churches met with devastating rejection.

In 1978 the mass suicide at Jonestown added new horror to the word *cult*. Capitalizing on the opportunity, the publishers of both *The God-Men* and *The Mindbenders* announced that their books would be released in second editions. Appeals by the local churches to authors and publishers again fell on deaf ears. In desperation, litigation was considered. There seemed no other avenue open for the local churches to respond. They considered the filing of a lawsuit as a modern "appeal to Caesar" (Acts 25:9-10), which the Apostle Paul had exercised when his life was threatened by the Jewish religionists of his day. The goal of the lawsuits was to make the truth known to the public and thus stop the unrelenting persecution. In 1980, after three years of frustrated attempts to correct grievous misrepresentation and after immense suffering, lawsuits for libel were filed against the two sister publications, *The Mindbenders* and *The God-Men*.

Those lawsuits became the forum to test the truth of the books' allegations. Detailed investigation and discovery was done on every issue. Sworn testimony of the people involved was recorded by deposition. Over two hundred volumes of sworn testimony were taken. Countless thousands of documents were produced and analyzed. Every libelous charge was examined in detail, as were all the persons involved. The writers and publishers had every opportunity to establish the truth of their accusations under oath; they had every opportunity to impeach the experts that would testify for the local churches. Later they would claim that because they did not have the opportunity to cross-examine the experts during the trial, the outcome was not reliable. The fact is, however, that they carried out their examination for over three years of depositions in preparation for the trial. Through that long examination their books were not vindicated; rather, the motive, malice, and deliberate distortion of the writers and publishers were exposed.

The six experts studied the church and the critical publications with the freedom to investigate in any way they wished. They read much of the sworn testimony of those involved in writing *The God-Men*. Some of the six attended the depositions of the witnesses and experts named to support the writers. Some gave detailed consideration to the testimony of hostile and critical ex-members of the local churches. The six men were prepared to deal with all the issues and present their conclusions in the face of hostile cross-examination.

The detailed and impartial conclusions of the six experts are overwhelming in their condemnation of *The God-Men* as a deliberate misrepresentation of the true beliefs and practices of Witness Lee and the local churches. The experts found the cult charge to be a fabrication of the authors. They found quotes consistently made to mean something opposite to what Witness Lee meant. They found "case studies" to be built upon unsubstantiated reports of persons of questionable motive. They found the trappings of social science used to give the book a false air of scholarship. The teachings of Witness Lee were taken from their Christian context and twisted to fit the cultic accusations.

After three years of discovery and deposition, the publisher of *The Mindbenders* withdrew the book from publication with an apology to Witness Lee and the local churches. That retraction was printed in major newspapers around the country on April 10, 1983. It is included here in the Appendix. The authors of *The Mindbenders* also signed the settlement agreement of which the retraction was a part. That legally ended publication and distribution of *The Mindbenders*.

The case against *The God-Men* was ready to go to trial in April 1985. However, just hours before the start of the trial SCP filed for reorganization under the protection of the bankruptcy court. Although they had an extensive base of support and had consistently raised funds during the discovery process, SCP claimed they could not afford to go to trial. This action allowed them to avoid the trial with a potentially large damage award and the cross-examination that had exposed the motive and methods of their work in the past three years of sworn testimony.

The God-Men's main author, Neil Duddy, separated himself from SCP and moved to Denmark. He did not appear at the trial. The Swiss publisher of the German edition, Schwengler-Verlag, also failed to appear. Thus, the trial was uncontested. Nevertheless, Judge Leon Seyranian took a very active role in questioning the witnesses concerning both the factual matters and the opinions of the experts. Despite the non-appearance of the defendants, the facts of the case and the conclusions of experts were presented before the court.

The 32-page Statement of Decision that resulted from the trial condemns the complete falsity of *The God-Men*. The facts referenced in detail by the judge come from the sworn testimony of the defendants as well as the experts. Those facts speak for themselves. The Court's opinion began:

> This matter came on regularly for trial and was heard as an uncontested matter.... Although the trial was uncontested, the Court feels that the plaintiffs have presented competent and reliable evidence, and the Court was very impressed with the stature and quality of the witnesses presented. Moreover, the Court was provided with a complete opportunity to question and cross examine the witnesses in order to ascertain the truth as the Court should do in a case involving First Amendment rights, regardless of whether the defendants appear or not. There was nothing that the Court wanted to see or to ask that was not provided. Furthermore, the evidence on behalf of the plaintiffs was substantiated by independent evidence from qualified expert witnesses. Accordingly, the Court finds that the manuscript by Neil T. Duddy, entitled *The God-Men* (Exhibit 1) disseminated (published) in the United States, the book *Die Sonderlehre des Witness Lee Und Seiner Ortsgemeinde* published by Schwengeler-Verlag (Exhibit 3) disseminated (published) in Europe, and the book *The God-Men, An Inquiry into Witness Lee and the Local Church* by Neil T. Duddy and the SCP published by Inter-Varsity Press (Exhibit 5) disseminated (published) in the United States and England, are in all major

respects false, defamatory and unprivileged, and, therefore, libelous. (California Civil Code §45)

The entire text of the Statement of Decision is available from this publisher.

The financial award of $11.9 million reflected the Judge's opinion of the damages done and his reaction to the malice involved in writing the book. However, none of the money awarded in that judgment was ever awarded to the plaintiffs. SCP reorganized under the court's supervision and went back into business.

The most valuable award of the court's action is the testimony recorded in this book. Although *The God-Men* and *The Mindbenders* were withdrawn from publication, the rumors they created linger on. With every new cult scare, the old, false information is repeated. The testimony of this book is an antidote to those accusations that are still being repeated.

Ten years after their testimony, the six experts found in this book remain firm in their conclusions concerning Witness Lee and the local churches. All have reviewed their testimony before the publication of this volume and had opportunity to make current comments. Dr. Melton tried to use his book *Encyclopedic Handbook of Cults in America,* published in 1993, as an opportunity to inform people of the wrong classification of the local churches that was initiated by these two books. Unfortunately, some assumed that his mere mention of the local churches in that book meant he had changed his mind and now considers the local churches a cult. A recent letter dated July 3, 1995, from Dr. Melton to a person in Japan who had made the same assumption, states his present position clearly:

> For a brief period in the early 1980s, a few people with a personal vendetta against the Local Church, accused it of being a cult. However, such accusations have proved unfounded and have not been heard here for almost a decade.
>
> I emphasize most strongly, that my inclusion of them in my book (as was clearly stated in the introduction) was solely to refute their likeness to the other groups discussed in the book. In North America, no literature has appeared in almost a decade which even hints at the Local Church being a "cult."

After several years of examination of them, I concluded that the Local Church was an orthodox Christian Church whose differences from other churches was primarily in matters of ecclesiology, piety, and eschatology, i.e. the same matters upon which all Christian denominations disagree and about which disagreement is allowed.

At last the public can consider the testimony of truly qualified experts and come to a proper conclusion concerning Witness Lee and the local churches. The issue here is not merely vindication of a person or group. Those in the local churches rejoice for an examination of the truth. If some readers can receive new light and inspiration concerning God's economy with man on this earth, all the labor has not been in vain. If some choose to disagree in the details of belief, it is still satisfying to know that the real belief of the local churches has finally been made more clear. To the great court of public opinion we commend this book. May your reading bring you the light, the freedom, and the joy that is found only in the truth.

Dan Towle
Anaheim, California
October 26, 1995

Chapter Two

THE TESTIMONY OF JOHN GORDON MELTON, Ph.D.

Mr. Morgan: *Doctor, I have marked as Exhibit 10 a curriculum vitae, and I will just ask if you can identify that.*
Dr. Melton: This is the curriculum vitae which I sent to you.
Mr. Morgan: *Is it up-to-date?*
Dr. Melton: Not quite.
> Mr. Morgan: *I will offer that into evidence, Your Honor.*
> Judge Seyranian: *May I see it for just a moment?*
> Mr. Morgan: *Certainly.*
> Judge Seyranian: *In evidence.*

Mr. Morgan: *Doctor, just a few questions about that. First, what is your present occupation?*
Dr. Melton: I am the director of the Institute for the Study of American Religion and the pastor of the Emmaus United Methodist Church in Chicago.
Mr. Morgan: *Can you tell us what the Institute for the Study of American Religion is?*
Dr. Melton: The Institute for the Study of American Religion is an independent research facility founded in 1969 for the purpose of studying, providing public information, and research on the smaller religious groups of America.
Mr. Morgan: *How long have you been involved in it?*
Dr. Melton: I was one of the founders.
Mr. Morgan: *Will you tell the court a little bit about your educational background so that the court will know what your qualifications are for this field?*
Dr. Melton: I have a Master of Divinity degree from Garrett Theological Seminary with a concentration in church history and a Ph.D. from Northwestern University in the history

and literature of religions with a specialty in American history.

MR. MORGAN: *Doctor, have you also done some teaching?*

DR. MELTON: I have taught at Garrett Theological Seminary and at several universities around the country. I have never held a teaching position up until just immediately in the future. I have just accepted a position with the University of California in Santa Barbara and am in the process right now of moving there.

MR. MORGAN: *What will you be teaching?*

DR. MELTON: Church history. I will be in their Religious Studies Department. My concentration will be in the area of minority religions in America.

MR. MORGAN: *Now you have listed in Exhibit 10 as publications the* Encyclopedia of American Religions. *Can you tell the court what that is?*

DR. MELTON: *Encyclopedia of American Religions* is the standard reference book surveying American religious groups.

MR. MORGAN: *I am holding up two volumes of it, and is that the book or the books?*

DR. MELTON: That's two-thirds of it. The third volume is ready to appear.

MR. MORGAN: *What is your function with this Encyclopedia?*

DR. MELTON: I am the author of it.

MR. MORGAN: *Just generally, what does the Encyclopedia purport to present to the reader?*

DR. MELTON: It presents a write-up on each of about 1,500 denominations, religious groups, currently alive and well in America. It presents their doctrines and beliefs in their historical context, how they are related to other religious groups.

MR. MORGAN: *You say you were the author. Can you tell the court what was the scope of the work you did in preparing this Encyclopedia?*

DR. MELTON: Well, up until the time it appeared, it had consumed most of my adult life. I did a great deal of research on it. I spent three years on the road gathering material for it. The actual writing took about five years.

MR. MORGAN: *Can you give the court some indication of the size of your library dealing with religious books?*
DR. MELTON: At the time the book appeared, my library was about 18,000 volumes. It is now about 25,000.
MR. MORGAN: *Doctor, there is just one other thing I wanted to ask you about the American Academy of Religion that you have indicated that you are a member of. What is that?*
DR. MELTON: The American Academy of Religion is the prime scholarly association for religious scholars.
MR. MORGAN: *Can one join it just by paying a membership fee or is there some criterion?*
DR. MELTON: You have to have academic credentials and pass a review board, as with most scholarly associations.
MR. MORGAN: *Fine. Doctor, do you know an organization entitled Spiritual Counterfeits Project?*
DR. MELTON: Yes.
MR. MORGAN: *How long have you been aware of that organization?*
DR. MELTON: Since its inception. I became aware of its predecessor organization, Christian World Liberation Front, in the early seventies.
MR. MORGAN: *And how well do you know the organization?*
DR. MELTON: Well, I followed its publications since I became aware of it around 1970, 1971. I have a fairly complete set of the material that they have published. I have visited with them. I know most of the leadership, some of them on a first-name basis.
MR. MORGAN: *Have you made a study of the history of SCP?*
DR. MELTON: Not particularly what we'd call a formal study. I have just been aware of it by receiving its publications, which I have read regularly for nine years.
    JUDGE SEYRANIAN: *Dr. Melton, are they listed in your Encyclopedia of American Religions?*
    DR. MELTON: No, they are not what I call a primary religious group. They are not a denomination. They are an organization made up of people who are members of other churches. They are not listed there.

JUDGE SEYRANIAN: *They are, in a sense, not a formal religion, per se?*
DR. MELTON: Right.
MR. MORGAN: *Let's talk about the "Local Church." Is the "Local Church" listed in your Encyclopedia?*
DR. MELTON: Oh, certainly.
MR. MORGAN: *Can you tell the court under what category it is listed?*
DR. MELTON: It is listed under what I call Independent Fundamentalist Churches and the subcategory under the Plymouth Brethren.
MR. MORGAN: *Can you explain to the court what you mean when you say Independent Fundamentalists?*
DR. MELTON: Well, fundamentalism is the thought world that runs through much of the evangelical church in America. Mainline Christianity in America is the evangelical movement. The main part of that movement grew out of the British movement called the Plymouth Brethren, started by a man named John Nelson Darby.

Both Watchman Nee and Witness Lee, who are among the founders of what we call the "Local Church" here, were formerly members of one branch of the Plymouth Brethren, so the thought world is very much the same.
MR. MORGAN: *Let me go back to SCP now. Could you give the court a brief history of how it came into being?*
DR. MELTON: Christian World Liberation Front was originally a part of the Jesus People Movement in the San Francisco Bay area. It started in Southern California and spread up the coast.

That movement had a crisis in the mid-seventies and split into several factions, one part of which became what today we know as the Evangelical Orthodox Church. Another part became the Berkeley Christian Coalition, and SCP was a part of the Berkeley Christian Coalition and gradually emerged as the dominant part, as the Christian Coalition faded away.
MR. MORGAN: *The Evangelical Orthodox Church you referred to, was there some individual who was a leader?*
DR. MELTON: Jack Sparks is the prime one who is known as

the continuing person. He was a very prominent leader of Christian World Liberation Front and is one of the bishops of the Evangelical Orthodox Church.

MR. MORGAN: *Let's talk about SCP again. What does SCP represent to be its purpose or function in this country?*

DR. MELTON: SCP carries on a function that the Christian World Liberation Front had begun before it, namely to become Christian apologists on the campus where a number of different alternative religions had arisen to do evangelism. They were trying to do Christian apologetics, both to refute the teachings of non-Christian groups and to present Christianity in a light that was both evangelical and acceptable intellectually in a campus situation.

MR. MORGAN: *Can you explain the term* apologetics?

DR. MELTON: The traditional sense of apology, of presenting your teachings in a most attractive way to your audience and explaining to them clearly.

MR. MORGAN: *At some point did SCP become known as an anti-cult organization?*

DR. MELTON: As the SCP grew and became affiliated with other groups that are also doing Christian apologetics in this area, in general, they took on a popular image as an anti-cult group. There are a number of Christian ministries that are also engaged in Christian apologetics in this area. Those ministries have become associated, in the public mind, with secular groups which arose during the mid 1970s and are generally all lumped together as anti-cult.

MR. MORGAN: *Can you give the court some indication as to the visibility or the awareness of the religious public about SCP? Is it well known?*

DR. MELTON: SCP is one of the two or three best-known groups who are working in this area. They are not the oldest by any means and probably not the single best known, but they are certainly one of the best known, and their reputation has been built upon the quality of their material. The quality has been much higher than most of the groups working in this area.

JUDGE SEYRANIAN: *Doctor, if I may ask you, where did*

they get the word Counterfeits Project? How did that happen to get in their name? Do you know?

DR. MELTON: It is part of theological jargon. The idea is that non-Christian religions are a counterfeit product of the devil, of God's true religion, and their project is to define and refute the counterfeit and present the truth. It is a theological term. It does not carry, at least in the theological jargon, the connotation that the people involved in the other religion are frauds or putting out fake money. It is a spiritual counterfeit. One of the problems that they have is that most people are not aware of that jargon.

JUDGE SEYRANIAN: *So the name in effect refers to what they are so-called fighting against rather than what they believe in themselves.*

DR. MELTON: Right.

JUDGE SEYRANIAN: *The counterfeit part is what they oppose.*

DR. MELTON: Right.

MR. MORGAN: *Has it been your observation that to the average person, when SCP goes against a particular organization, the person then envisages that organization as a counterfeit or a fraud?*

DR. MELTON: That's been some of the problems with SCP all along.

MR. MORGAN: *Has it been your observation that when SCP goes after an organization, they are given a lot of credence; in other words, people accept what they say about organizations?*

DR. MELTON: Right. SCP has overall, through the last decade, done the best work in this area. The quality of some of their books is quite good. Their book on Reverend Moon, their book on Buddhism, and their book on Holistic Health, these have all been quite well received; and they are, from an evangelical Christian point of view, excellent books.

MR. MORGAN: *Can you make the same statement for the books that are the subject of this lawsuit?*

DR. MELTON: No, I can't.

MR. MORGAN: *Let me digress for a moment. Can you tell the court when you first became aware of the "Local Church"?*

DR. MELTON: I first became aware of it in the early seventies when I was still in seminary. I discovered some of Watchman Nee's materials and purchased them in a Christian book store.

MR. MORGAN: *What is it about Watchman Nee's material that attracted you?*

DR. MELTON: I originally was attracted because I had never heard of it, and I just bought one of his books to read it, to see who he was, what he was all about. The book had an intriguing title, *The Normal Christian Church Life*, and I was pastoring a small church at that time. I wanted to see what he had to say. It was shortly after that I became aware that he was also the leader-founder of another movement.

MR. MORGAN: *Can you give the court some indication of the acceptance of Watchman Nee's writings in the United States?*

DR. MELTON: Watchman Nee's writings are fairly well accepted. Most Christian bookstores still carry his writings to this day.

MR. MORGAN: *How about Watchman Nee? Did you make any study of him?*

DR. MELTON: Eventually, I tracked down a biography of his life, actually several books about him, and, yes, I made a study in preparation for the article on the "Local Church" for the Encyclopedia.

MR. MORGAN: *Can you tell the court briefly the history of Watchman Nee as you observed it?*

DR. MELTON: Watchman Nee was a third-generation Christian; his grandfather was a Congregationalist minister in China. He grew up in a Christian home, went through his adolescent rebellion period, but then professed conversion. He then became associated with a number of people who had broken away from the formal Christian missions in China and were operating as independent evangelical Christians.

As he continued to move in those circles, he eventually encountered the Plymouth Brethren and became affiliated with them. They brought him to England where he fellowshipped with a branch of the so-called Exclusive Plymouth Brethren.

As he was wandering around, he began to fellowship with some other evangelists, people who had in the nineteenth century been associated with the Brethren but had broken away. Because of his association with them, the Exclusive Brethren broke their tie with him. At that point he became fully independent because he was back in China and he was not geographically close to the other independent evangelicals except through their books, and he began his own movement.

He also, at that time, developed several peculiar ideas that were kind of exclusive to him, the main one being the idea of the local church, that the unity of Christianity, which was a problem on the mission field because there were so many different groups, was best established by a New Testament principle, as he put it, of having only one church in each geographic location or each city. That is how the group eventually got its name. It was a name put on it rather than one that it had accepted.

MR. MORGAN: *What happened to Watchman Nee?*

DR. MELTON: After World War II he was arrested by the communists because of some of his activities, and he spent the rest of his life in prison. He died in the early seventies in a prison.

MR. MORGAN: *Did you also learn about any relationship between Witness Lee and Watchman Nee?*

DR. MELTON: Witness Lee had also been a member of the Brethren and had been attracted to Watchman Nee's movement. I think in part because it was an indigenous movement rather than a missionary movement. He joined it, became an elder and a leader in the movement, and eventually became one of Watchman Nee's right-hand men, so to speak, and was sent by Nee to work with the churches in Taiwan.

MR. MORGAN: *You have told us that was your first experience with the "Local Church." Did you ever have an occasion to actually come to meet an actual "Local Church"?*

DR. MELTON: In 1972 the "Local Church" became an object of interest in some of the evangelical press in Chicago. I discovered there was a congregation there and over the next several years attended it on a number of occasions. It was on those occasions I first became aware of Witness Lee, purchased some of his books and read them, and gathered the material that allowed me to write the item in the Encyclopedia.

MR. MORGAN: *You mentioned purchasing books. Was there some facility for that?*

DR. MELTON: They had a book table, a literature rack, and I purchased some. I don't know exactly when, but within a few years they had opened up a Bible and book store which is still in existence in Chicago, a very fine Christian bookstore. They have a wide variety of Christian evangelical material, and being an evangelical myself, I have stopped in regularly and purchased items.

MR. MORGAN: *You used a term in talking about Watchman Nee of fellowship. Can you explain to the court how that term is being used by you and people generally in the evangelical field?*

DR. MELTON: Well, it has a peculiar meaning among the Brethren. To fellowship means that you are essentially in communion with them, that you go on Sunday and break bread. You can participate in the Lord's supper, and among the Brethren that is a sign that you are accepted, that you are allowed to fellowship at the Lord's table.

The problem that Watchman Nee had is that he went over to Austin-Spark's church, and he fellowshipped with Austin-Sparks. He broke bread with them. And when the Exclusive Brethren found out about that, they would not break bread with anyone who also broke bread with Austin-Sparks.

MR. MORGAN: *Okay.*

JUDGE SEYRANIAN: *Is Austin-Sparks related to Jack Sparks at all?*

DR. MELTON: No. It is Austin dash Sparks, he's Austin-Sparks. That is his last name. He is a Britisher, and he is dead now.

MR. MORGAN: *Now, did you at our request, in the latter part of last year and in preparation for the trial of this matter, undertake to do certain projects for us?*

DR. MELTON: Yes, you asked me to look over Duddy's book in some depth and to evaluate it.

MR. MORGAN: *Did we also ask you to make any evaluation of the "Local Church" and Witness Lee's writings?*

DR. MELTON: At the same time the two projects went hand in hand. You had to do one to do the other, and I was also invited to come to California and to see some of the local churches in action there.

MR. MORGAN: *Incidentally, prior to our requesting that, had you seen Mr. Duddy's book,* The God-Men?

DR. MELTON: I purchased a copy soon after it came out and read part of it, skimmed through it, and put it on the shelf. It was not a matter of particular concern at that time.

MR. MORGAN: *Will you tell the court what you did by way of performing the assignment that we asked you to do?*

DR. MELTON: I attended some more "Local Church" meetings in Chicago to see that they were still doing what they were doing in the mid-seventies when I had attended a number of times. I attended some house fellowships. I did the same on a stay in California and also toured the offices of Living Stream. I went over one Saturday morning to see a work session for the members that gathered to clean the church and had a short devotional period before that.

I read more of Witness Lee's books than I ever thought I would have to and plowed through sets of periodicals from the various "Local Church" congregations as well as other publications from different "Local Churches." I read a set of material from Bill Freeman's ministry in Seattle. It amounted to about six feet of books that I plowed through as well as going through Mr. Duddy's transcript.

MR. MORGAN: *Did you also have an occasion to look at some videotapes?*

DR. MELTON: I looked at a whole set of videotapes that were supplied to me. There were six in number. They were anywhere from an hour to two hours in length. That's been my major contact. I have never met Witness Lee, but I did see him on tape.

MR. MORGAN: *These tapes, were they of meetings where Witness Lee participated?*

DR. MELTON: Most of them were, yes. They covered a wide variety of sessions; sometimes he was lecturing, and sometimes he was interacting with the audience, doing various things.

MR. MORGAN: *Did these tapes also show the members of the church?*

DR. MELTON: Right. The members were always there, pictures of them, and there was one tape in particular where the major part of the tape had the members interacting with Witness Lee.

MR. MORGAN: *And were these tapes purporting to be back in the 1970s.*

DR. MELTON: They covered several years. I don't remember the exact dates, but they went from the mid seventies seemingly into the late seventies.

MR. MORGAN: *All right, fine. After completing that study, what opinion, if any, did you form regarding Witness Lee and the "Local Church"?*

DR. MELTON: The same opinion I had at the time that I wrote the Encyclopedia article, that Witness Lee was a variety of the Plymouth Brethren, that it very much fit into that stream of Independent Fundamentalist Christian history, and that it was an orthodox evangelical group. As an evangelical, I think the main opinion was that I don't have any problem fellowshipping with him.

MR. MORGAN: *When you use the term* orthodox, *can you tell the court what is meant by that?*

DR. MELTON: It means that they hold to the basic orthodox statements of Christian faith concerning God, Christ, and the Holy Spirit. They believe the Bible to be the word of God.

MR. MORGAN: *Now let's go to Mr. Duddy's work,* The God-Men. *Did you form any opinions of that work?*

DR. MELTON: I formed the overall opinion that Mr. Duddy had completely misunderstood what was happening in the "Local Church" and had completely misrepresented both their history and their beliefs and their practices.

MR. MORGAN: *What is the significance of misrepresenting the history of the church?*

DR. MELTON: Essentially Duddy's history of the church begins in the 1920s when Watchman Nee formed his own independent movement. There is no mention of his prior affiliation with the Brethren or any mention of his taking over from the Brethren their long history, the major part of their doctrine, or any understanding of how Witness Lee and the "Local Church" see themselves historically as fitting into the mainstream of evangelical Christian history.

This in effect cuts them off from the Christian tradition that they are very much a part of, and he presents them as something new and different. While they have a couple of differences, the overwhelming amount of their church belief and their church life is taken directly out of the mainstream of evangelical thought.

JUDGE SEYRANIAN: *I want to ask a question, Doctor. In reading* The God-Men, *did you check some of the material that was stated there to see whether or not the statements, as made, were true or not?*

DR. MELTON: No, I did not. The first time that I read *The God-Men* I was involved in some other projects. I got it; I read it. I read the biography of Watchman Nee that Angus Kinnear had written, and there is another book on Watchman Nee that a fellow named Roberts had written. Reading *The God-Men,* the presentation in the early chapters was shallow. As I got into the book I recognized some of this just didn't fit with my experience, but I didn't have time to check it out, so I just put it on the shelf.

MR. MORGAN: *What I think the court is asking is, when you started to do the work for us, did you do that?*

DR. MELTON: Oh, I have read the book three or four times.

JUDGE SEYRANIAN: *What I am saying is, "It is your testimony that there are certain statements in* The God-Men *book that are not correct regarding the 'Local Church.'"*

DR. MELTON: Yes.

JUDGE SEYRANIAN: *Did you do anything actively to check those statements to verify whether they were true or not?*

DR. MELTON: Oh, yes. Over the past year I have gone

through *The God-Men* in some depth, taking individual statements and checking them against Witness Lee's material.

MR. MORGAN: Let me ask you a couple of questions before I get to specifics here. You have mentioned that Mr. Duddy, in addition to misrepresenting the history, has misrepresented the beliefs and practices. Can you tell the court just in a general way, and then we will get into the specifics, in what way Mr. Duddy misrepresented the beliefs and practices?

DR. MELTON: Mr. Duddy has fairly consistently taken statements, usually individual sentences from the middle of paragraphs, out of context and made them to appear to say things that they were not even talking about.

He has done that consistently through the book. He has misrepresented the piety of the "Local Church," most particularly in terms of the pray-reading, which is one form of prayer in the "Local Church," and has presented it as a kind of an Eastern form of mantric prayer. He has not understood the organization of the "Local Church," which they took over from the Plymouth Brethren and which no one has ever questioned, though it is much more autocratic in the Plymouth Brethren than it is here. He has turned it into kind of a hierarchy, which doesn't really exist. So in those ways, overall, he's misrepresented it.

Primarily, underlying all of this is that Witness Lee is a teacher-preacher. He speaks extemporaneously at best from notes. In looking at the tapes, he will frequently stop and make a point that does not seem to even be in his notes, that he just all of a sudden thought up that he needed to make at this point.

Like most preachers, he speaks with images, and he speaks with hyperbole. He overstates cases to make a point and particularly with hyperboles, as any preacher, you can pull them out, put them in another context, and make them appear to be quite opposite of what Witness Lee was talking about. Witness Lee has a theology which underlies his thought, but it is not readily evident because he is preaching to lay people most of the time. He does not preach theology. He is not a great theologian or a systematic theologian, so his theology is not readily evident and he does not speak in abstract theological terms.

Very rarely does he talk theology as, say, a seminary professor would talk it. It does not mean he does not believe it. I get up on Sunday morning to preach to my people. I don't give them a lecture on the abstract doctrine of the Trinity. It is not particularly relevant to what they are going to do that afternoon.

JUDGE SEYRANIAN: *Mr. Morgan, will there be some of the material that is presented in* The God-Men *and how that has been taken out of context?*

MR. MORGAN: *Absolutely, Your Honor, with this witness and other witnesses also.*

JUDGE SEYRANIAN: *I'd be interested in hearing that.*

MR. MORGAN: *We will get to that very quickly, Your Honor. One more thing. Is there any thrust in Mr. Duddy's work that the "Local Church" is a cult?*

DR. MELTON: The thrust is twofold. In the introduction there is the discussion of the cult problem. It is left undecisive. It raises the issue, is it a cult or not? We are not ready to decide. The real problem is that SCP is identified as an anti-cult organization, and any group that they treat in depth is going to be identified in the public mind as a cult group, and if you go to Christian bookstores, where the book was sold, where I purchased it was at the Moody bookstore in Chicago, and it was on the shelf of books plainly marked as anti-cult books.

MR. MORGAN: *Can you explain to the court the dilemma of a group such as the "Local Church" when it is called a cult as to how it can erase that charge?*

DR. MELTON: It is very, very difficult. It is like opening up a pillow to the wind and then trying to reclaim all the feathers. It is a very difficult thing to do. They will be a long time, at best, erasing that image.

MR. MORGAN: *Is one of the problems that cults are claimed to be deceitful?*

DR. MELTON: Cults are claimed to be deceitful. They are claimed to be harmful to their members. They are claimed to be undermining American values. Cults are claimed to be just about every bad thing in the book these days, and with the pervasive images of Manson and Jim Jones hanging over us, any group that is called a cult is immediately associated with those two people.

JUDGE SEYRANIAN: *What is your definition of a cult?*

DR. MELTON: My working definition of a cult is a group that you don't like, and I say that somewhat facetiously, but at the same time, in fact, that is my working definition of a cult. It is a group that somebody doesn't like. It is a derogatory term, and I have never seen it redeemed from the derogatory connotations that it picked up in the sociological literature in the 1930s.

MR. MORGAN: *Has the term* cult *gone through all sorts of changes?*

DR. MELTON: It began as a sociological term in the twenties and thirties. It was used to describe leftover groups after sociologists had talked about churches and sects. They were a group that just didn't fit, and they were termed cults. They were treated primarily as esoterica in American religion.

Then in the thirties Christian apologists picked up the term and used it to describe groups that were either not orthodox in their theology or were not Christian at all. That became the most popular use of the term up until the 1970s.

Then in the seventies the secular anti-cult movement came along. America has experienced a great pluralism and a marked jump in pluralism in religion, and it has come to mean something actively destructive, not just something wrong but something destructive, psychologically so.

MR. MORGAN: *When a group like the "Local Church" protests and says, "We are not a cult," does that fall on deaf ears?*

DR. MELTON: Most of the time it does.

MR. MORGAN: *And is that because the charge had been made that they are deceitful?*

DR. MELTON: That is one of the reasons. Certainly in the case of the "Local Church," the charge has been made that there are two levels of theology: a public theology and a private theology. If you have a public theology that seems to be somewhat acceptable, but people say, "Well, your private theology is not acceptable" and "This is what you really believe," then it is very difficult to deal with that.

MR. MORGAN: *In your study of the "Local Church," have you found any evidence of two different theologies in the church?*

DR. MELTON: No. The material that is given to leaders in the church is published, available to anyone, and is sold and marketed quite freely.

MR. MORGAN: *Are most of Witness Lee's teachings reduced to writing?*

DR. MELTON: Overwhelmingly. Within a very short time, much of his material first appears in a pamphlet form and circulates as individual pamphlets and then is compiled into books. Almost all of his books are transcripts of his talks.

JUDGE SEYRANIAN: *Is* The God-Men *entirely devoted to the "Local Church"?*

DR. MELTON: Yes.

JUDGE SEYRANIAN: *The book is approximately how many pages long? I haven't seen it.*

DR. MELTON: A couple of hundred.

JUDGE SEYRANIAN: *Is there anything in the book that you would say is accurate and some portions that are not accurate, or would you say the book totally seems to misstate the principles of the "Local Church"?*

DR. MELTON: There are certainly some accurate statements in the book, but overall the book totally misrepresents the thought. I don't think Mr. Duddy ever understood Lee's theology.

Lee is basically a dispensationalist. That idea is never presented in the book. If you are going to do a picture of Lee's theology and not discuss dispensationalism, I don't see how you can do it.

JUDGE SEYRANIAN: *Does Duddy say he wrote this book based on his readings of Lee's writings, or is it based on being a member of the church?*

DR. MELTON: He wrote it based upon his study of the church and reading a number of Lee's books, which are footnoted in the back.

JUDGE SEYRANIAN: *Does he ever, to your knowledge, claim that he attended their meetings and their sessions?*

DR. MELTON: Yes, on several occasions.

JUDGE SEYRANIAN: *He says that?*

DR. MELTON: Not in the book but in his deposition.

MR. MORGAN: *You have had an opportunity to review his deposition also, have you not?*

DR. MELTON: Yes.

MR. MORGAN: *Let's go first to a paragraph from* The God-Men I, *where it says:*

> Witness Lee's statements reveal that the Local Church's use of "the name of the Lord" stands clearly in this same tradition and is technological and pagan rather than biblical and Christian.

First, what is Mr. Duddy purporting to say to the readers there?

DR. MELTON: He is purporting to say that a particular prayer practice of the "Local Church" is likened to an Eastern technique of spiritual growth.

In a number of Eastern religions, the structure is such that the individual goes to a guru, and the guru gives him one or more techniques which he is to practice over and over and over again, and those techniques become a means of altering the consciousness and of eventually receiving mystical enlightenment. That is what a guru does.

MR. MORGAN: *That doesn't play any part in Christian prayer, does it?*

DR. MELTON: There are within the monastic tradition and within Eastern orthodoxy guru-like structures. If you joined a contemplative order, you would have among the people you associated with a spiritual director who would often-times give you disciplines and practices to help you to gain a mystical oneness with God.

MR. MORGAN: *Let's talk in terms of evangelicals.*

DR. MELTON: In evangelicalism, that kind of practice has been looked upon with great disdain, and within evangelicalism you would not find that practice.

MR. MORGAN: *In the evangelical religion would it be considered as non-Christian?*

DR. MELTON: Certainly in many branches of evangelicalism.

Among the majority of evangelicals, the practice of a kind of Eastern discipline would be very much looked upon with askance. Even meditation is looked upon with some askance.

MR. MORGAN: *Let me ask you. The prayer practices of the "Local Church," are they technological and pagan?*

DR. MELTON: No, they are not. The main prayer practices of calling upon the name of the Lord and pray-reading are quite vocal, quite communal. They involve the use of the mental faculties in a way that the prayer practices, say, of Hinduism do not, which are designed to quiet the mind and alter consciousness.

If one participated in a pray-reading session, for example, it is very loud, very boisterous; people are jumping up and down. They are communicating with each other through their words. The words take on a great deal of importance.

You have to stay in a fairly normal state of consciousness to participate in this. Unlike, say, for example, a mantra in Hinduism, where you repeat a word over and over again, and it alters your consciousness and puts you into a meditative state. That doesn't happen. It is quite the opposite of pray-reading.

MR. MORGAN: *If Mr. Duddy had in fact studied the "Local Church," as he represented, and attended meetings, is there any basis for him making that statement?*

DR. MELTON: The only basis is that in pray-reading and calling upon the name of the Lord, certain words are repeated more than one time. That is the only slim thread of connection. The whole atmosphere of pray-reading and the dynamics of the group at the time it is done are just completely different. You could not meditate while pray-reading was going on.

MR. MORGAN: *Is there any basis, then, for saying it is technological and pagan?*

DR. MELTON: No, it is spontaneous. When you start pray-reading, you don't know what is going to happen by the time it is over with.

MR. MORGAN: *Is this something that Mr. Duddy, in your opinion, could misunderstand, or is he doing something else?*

DR. MELTON: It is something he could misunderstand because as far as I can tell, he's not done any study of Eastern religions. The attempt to equate pray-reading with Eastern mantric practices has been something that has appeared in writing by other authors in SCP literature. He could have misunderstood it, but he certainly had no knowledge of what he wrote; that is, he could have misunderstood it. He could have deliberately misrepresented it at this point, but he had not done any study of Eastern religions in order to make this kind of statement.

JUDGE SEYRANIAN: *At the time did the SCP only write books regarding cults, or did they just do general religious articles?*

DR. MELTON: No. That is primarily their only literature. At the time that they were founded, Your Honor, they were one segment of a group that had five or six compartments, and other compartments were writing other kinds of literature of a more general nature. SCP had a special task assigned to it.

JUDGE SEYRANIAN: *It is like a mission that they had?*

DR. MELTON: Right, that was their mission. As they have emerged as a separate organization, they have continued that mission, and among Christian evangelicals there are over a hundred groups like SCP that have that one mission and see themselves doing that one thing. Some of them are even specialized to the point that they do literature only on one group, such as Mormonism or Jehovah's Witnesses or one of the other larger groups.

JUDGE SEYRANIAN: *When they are attacking, and you use the word* cult *as the way they attack them, is that your original definition or more modern definition? The original one was, "Anything I dislike or bothers me."*

DR. MELTON: That is a modern one.

JUDGE SEYRANIAN: *They are using the modern definition of a cult, is that correct?*

DR. MELTON: No, their definition of a cult is a group that either is non-Christian in its teachings or is an unacceptable variation of Christianity because of its doctrinal deviation from orthodoxy.

JUDGE SEYRANIAN: *Do psychological forms of the religion have anything to do with whether they are a cult or not, in other words, whether they work on your mind, either captivate you, control you, or control your actions?*

DR. MELTON: In the best of the traditional literature since the thirties, no, it doesn't. It is strictly a doctrinal matter. Since around 1974 as the secular anti-cult groups have emerged, psychological issues have come to the fore, and unfortunately some of the Christian groups have always accepted those kinds of psychological and pop-sociological observations as additional ways to attack the cult.

MR. MORGAN: *Can you explain a little more about that? Can you give us an example of that?*

DR. MELTON: Well, when the secular anti-cult movement emerged in the early seventies, it began to attack groups such as the Unification Church and the Children of God. The secular anti-cult movement quickly saw that it wanted to take court action and that religious issues had little or no effect in court.

So they developed a hypothesis that those groups were brainwashing the members. They were deceitfully recruiting them and brainwashing them, and what has happened is that hypothesis has come into some of the Christian literature. The Christian counter-cult ministries and secular anti-cultists saw themselves as fighting a common enemy at times, and on a very personal level have developed relationships and networks. That secular thought world has now entered the Christian counter-cult literature, which was at its best purely doctrinal polemics.

JUDGE SEYRANIAN: *Does SCP, when fighting or attacking cults in their writings, refer to those groups that in a sense do a certain amount of brainwashing of their members?*

DR. MELTON: SCP in its literature has primarily been doctrinal, but at various points it has also said that not only is this group doctrinally wrong; it is also psychologically harmful, and it has in certain places brought in the secular critic of cults to supplement its attack on specific groups.

JUDGE SEYRANIAN: *Then their biggest objection is more doctrinal than it is brainwashing?*
DR. MELTON: Overall, it has been.
JUDGE SEYRANIAN: *Well, now with respect to a doctrinal attack to these groups, is it certain teachings that these groups maintain that they oppose? In other words, is it some fundamental stream that runs through these groups that they seem to oppose?*
DR. MELTON: Yes.
JUDGE SEYRANIAN: *What is that?*
DR. MELTON: Their opinion of the Bible.
JUDGE SEYRANIAN: *No, wait. These cult groups, are they based basically on the teachings of the Bible too?*
DR. MELTON: There are a set of them that profess to be Christian and to derive their teachings from the Bible.

For example, Mormons profess to believe the Bible. But Mormons are attacked because not only do they believe the Bible, but they put beside it a second and third revelation, namely, the *Book of Mormon*, the *Pearl of Great Price* and the *Doctrine and Covenants*. These are seen as equal in authority with Scripture just as *Science and Health* is seen as equal in authority by Christian Scientists.

Evangelicals would attack these groups, if attack is the right term, I think it is, based on their doctrine of the Bible. Their understanding of the Bible is faulty because they put beside the Bible something else of equal worth, so that any group that questions the absolute and unique authority of the Bible would be subject to critique by evangelicals.

JUDGE SEYRANIAN: *So the SCP technically could attack the Mormon Church.*
DR. MELTON: And do.
JUDGE SEYRANIAN: *It would be, in your opinion, like an attack on a cult in a sense.*
DR. MELTON: Oh, yes. The Mormons are a classic cult. They are one of the groups that were used to define the term *cult* originally.
JUDGE SEYRANIAN: *Oh, really?*
DR. MELTON: Yes. The Mormons, Christian Scientists,

Seventh-day Adventists, Theosophy, Spiritualism, and Jehovah's Witnesses. Those were the original cults in the 1930s.

MR. MORGAN: *That was when you were dealing strictly with doctrine, right?*

DR. MELTON: Right.

MR. MORGAN: *That has evolved to where a cult now is something equivalent to a Jonestown?*

DR. MELTON: That is the extreme.

JUDGE SEYRANIAN: *Jonestown was the brainwashing type, wasn't it?*

DR. MELTON: That's right.

JUDGE SEYRANIAN: *If anybody can get people to kill themselves, I suppose there is a certain amount of brainwashing, because isn't there something about all of us that has a will to live, will to survive; and then you have to overcome that, don't you?*

DR. MELTON: I don't know that I am the best one to speak to that, but I think there are a number of incidents where apart from brainwashing, just by a social conditioning, a group could accept that their best means of survival is bodily death.

We have seen it quite recently in Lebanon. The people who blew up the embassy there drove a truck in. They willingly committed suicide. That was their means of immortality.

JUDGE SEYRANIAN: *So they believe that they move on to the next life?*

DR. MELTON: Right, but it takes a certain community training over a period of time to do that.

JUDGE SEYRANIAN: *Does it take brainwashing to do that?*

DR. MELTON: I would not call it brainwashing. I would call it social conditioning. I have been socially conditioned all my life to put my life on the line if my country was threatened. I was taught, and I believe, that if this country was threatened and my life stood between it and its survival, I would be willing to give my life for its survival and put on a uniform and go do my thing. That is a matter of training from the time that one grows up in values and what is valuable.

JUDGE SEYRANIAN: *Do all the evangelical groups look upon certain of these groups, such as Mormons, Jehovah's Witnesses, and the others, and all classify them as cults?*

DR. MELTON: Yes.

JUDGE SEYRANIAN: *That is not something unique with SCP?*

DR. MELTON: No.

JUDGE SEYRANIAN: *Has that definition of what is a cult continued to the present day or is that the old teaching?*

DR. MELTON: It's grown. As I say, during the thirties you could find four or five books. During the fifties you could find fifteen or twenty books. Today you can go to any Christian bookstore and find two or three shelves of books under anti-cult materials.

JUDGE SEYRANIAN: *What I am trying to understand is what the average person believes, who is not familiar with theology and maybe the teachings of the evangelical church, when you refer to some of the cults you are talking about: the Moonies and the Mansons and the Jim Joneses and so forth. But as I understand what you are telling me now, it goes beyond that into a doctrinal teaching type of thing, and some of these other churches fall within that same definition as far as the evangelical people are concerned, just as Lee is labeled a cult. Whether that is bad or good is to be questioned.*

DR. MELTON: This is the situation we are into. Up until 1970, let's say, there was a set of Christian literature aimed at a specific set of around twenty-five or thirty organizations that were labeled cult, and it very plainly stated that by cult we mean those groups that deny the essentials of the Christian faith and are operating in the United States and in the West.

During the 1970s the secular anti-cult movement, the deprogramming movement grew up, became nationally based, and received a tremendous amount of publicity, especially in the late seventies after the Manson and Jonestown incidents. They have created a pervasive image of what a cult is in popular culture.

The Christian anti-cultists have continued to produce the

doctrinal material. In part, they have absorbed the additional polemics of the secular anti-cultists. In the public mind they cannot be separated from each other. For the public to go buy a Christian anti-cult book and to buy secular anti-cult books, there is very little way to tell the difference unless you are thoroughly specialized and understand what you are buying and reading. They are frequently on the shelf right next to each other.

JUDGE SEYRANIAN: *So on this shelf you talked about in Chicago where you found* The God-Men, *you could find books about the Mormon Church and Jehovah's Witnesses?*

DR. MELTON: Half of the books there were about Mormons or Jehovah's Witnesses, which are the two prime targets of anti-cult literature.

The rest would cover everything from the Moonies to the Hare Krishnas, the Children of God, and then this one.

JUDGE SEYRANIAN: *Let me just ask one other question. Would the SCP be an evangelical group? Do they call themselves an evangelical group?*

DR. MELTON: Yes.

JUDGE SEYRANIAN: *And again the definition of an evangelical group is what?*

DR. MELTON: A group that flows out of the Protestant Reformation and accepts the basic teachings of the Bible as their authority and is orthodox according to the Chalcedonian Creeds, the early creeds of the church, and is literally evangelical. That is, it is out to try to gain converts.

JUDGE SEYRANIAN: *Is the evangelical group as compared to other groups more heavily influenced by the Bible? In other words, is their teaching centered around the Bible exclusively?*

DR. MELTON: They are the people of the Book.

JUDGE SEYRANIAN: *Now, with respect to these other groups that we have mentioned as cults, the Mormons, the Jehovah's Witnesses, the Moonies' Unification Church, do they all have some connection claiming that they are Christian and that they have some connection with the Bible?*

DR. MELTON: Some do and some don't. You have one group of them, Unification Church, Children of God, that would fit into that. Christian Science and the Mormons, who claimed Christianity as their own but put beside the Bible other materials of equal authority. Then there is a second set, Hare Krishnas, Transcendental Meditation, Zen Buddhism, which make no claims to being Christian but have a complete alternative revelation.

JUDGE SEYRANIAN: *I appreciate all you are saying because I am getting a world of education.*

MR. MORGAN: *Doctor, let me go then to the book itself,* The God-Men. *Was there an attempt in that book to go beyond just doctrinal concepts?*

DR. MELTON: Oh, certainly. There was an attempt to attack the "Local Church" for psychological manipulation, to question its financial dealings.

MR. MORGAN: *These attacks on the psychological manipulation, that is just the very thing his Honor was talking about that people think in terms of a cult, that they are manipulating the minds of the people, is that right?*

DR. MELTON: Yes.

MR. MORGAN: *And did you find that those kind of statements by Mr. Duddy were false as they relate to the "Local Church?"*

DR. MELTON: I could find no evidence of it. The leadership of the church at one level, in terms of those who have independent ministries, such as Witness Lee and Bill Freeman, operates outside of the local congregations. They perform ministries which the local congregations then make use of.

The local congregations then buy their literature and attend their conferences. For example, Witness Lee would not be able to go into a local congregation and do anything locally in the affairs of that congregation.

The local congregations are run by elders, usually anywhere from two to five elders at any given local congregation. The mere fact that there are so few elders limits any ability they have to do any manipulation. If you are going to be manipulative, you have got to have more leaders to keep up with people over a period of time.

The church in Chicago with four or five elders has three or four hundred members. You just cannot keep up with people day after day and control their lives if you have that few leaders.

I might also add that there has been developed in the church a tremendous amount of lay responsibility. Their offices and functions are being turned over all the time so that people are always moving in and out of leadership positions in the local church administratively in terms of running the building and doing the affairs of the local church, and in Chicago handling the bookstore matters. So it is always changing so that no hierarchy gets established.

JUDGE SEYRANIAN: *I don't know exactly how you did your investigation. It would seem to me to be a difficult task, not being a member of the church where you are day to day, week to week, year to year, where you would know for yourself because you have been a member. And you are given this task to try and interpret a book and decide whether it is valid or not valid. Your job was a difficult one; I appreciate that.*

But on the other hand, just briefly from what I have heard, some of the things that Mr. Duddy is relying on are some dissidents who left the church and apparently are dissatisfied.

In your investigation did you also check with these people to see whether these are in fact true dissidents that have a gripe for some reason, or maybe there are two sides to every story? Like in a dissolution you hear the husband's side of the dissolution, and you can't see how he could live with her until you talk to the wife, and you find out that maybe he was equally at fault.

DR. MELTON: No, I did not have a chance to meet personally with ex-members.

MR. MORGAN: *To allay your thoughts, we have an expert who did just that.*

JUDGE SEYRANIAN: *You are reading my mind.*

DR. MELTON: It was one of my tasks, Your Honor, to take the testimony of ex-members that I was given and to check them against my experience.

JUDGE SEYRANIAN: *Okay.*

MR. MORGAN: *Let me ask you this. Is there some basic rule, though, in the field of religion about reliance upon ex-members?*

DR. MELTON: When you are investigating groups such as this, you never rely upon the unverified testimony of ex-members.

MR. MORGAN: *Why?*

DR. MELTON: To put it bluntly, hostile ex-members invariably shade the truth. They invariably blow out of proportion minor incidents and turn them into major incidents, and over a period of time their testimony almost always changes because each time they tell it they get the feedback of acceptance or rejection from those to whom they tell it, and hence it will be developed and merged into a different world view that they are adopting.

MR. MORGAN: *Let's go to the section "Spiritual Authority," and then we will go down a few sentences in the Duddy manuscript and it says:*

> *Reliable sources tell us that Lee himself does rule with an iron rod.*

First, what is the import of that statement? What is Mr. Duddy conveying to the reader?

DR. MELTON: That Witness Lee rules with an administrative authority that has real power and that he does it in a kingly sort of way, arbitrarily and at his own whim.

MR. MORGAN: *Is that some analogy to the psychological cults that we have been discussing?*

DR. MELTON: Later on as he begins to discuss psychological issues, a person who rules with an iron rod would be liked to an authoritarian guru who runs his disciples' lives.

MR. MORGAN: *How about a Jim Jones?*

DR. MELTON: Very much so.

MR. MORGAN: *Okay. Now, is that a correct statement?*

DR. MELTON: I have found no evidence to indicate that it is. Lee has a lot of authority within the church. Most of it is the authority that he has brought unto himself through years of people reading his books and listening to his teachings and accepting them. So he has earned his position by his labors over the years, and the respect and authority he has are primarily that.

His authority is at one level, that is as a teacher and as a trainer within the church. His authority is strictly limited in that he cannot go into a local congregation and begin to run the affairs of the "Local Church," and he has kept himself pretty much separated from being a congregational leader himself, so he does not have any direct leadership role over people.

MR. MORGAN: *Has Mr. Duddy then quoted from a couple of statements of Witness Lee on the next page, to sort of support his position?*

DR. MELTON: He has. He has built an argument on the next page that Lee is not only the leader of the church, but that he sees himself as God's oracle.

The import of seeing himself as God's oracle is twofold.

Number one, if you are speaking God's word, then your word carries authority, and you are an authoritarian figure who must be listened to.

Secondly, if you are speaking as God's oracle, you are putting your words as authority beside or above the Bible; therefore, you are moving yourself outside the evangelical camp by denying the absolute unique authority of the Scripture.

MR. MORGAN: *By oracle, could I reduce that to a simple term, that Mr. Duddy is representing that Mr. Lee is contending that he is God's mouthpiece?*

DR. MELTON: That is an apt paraphrase.

MR. MORGAN: *The two quotes on the next page made the representation that Witness Lee was saying that he was God's oracle or God's mouthpiece. Is that a fair and accurate representation of what Witness Lee is saying?*

DR. MELTON: No, it isn't.

MR. MORGAN: *Is it completely distorted?*

DR. MELTON: Completely.

MR. MORGAN: *Now can you tell the court where the quotes come from?*

DR. MELTON: In *The God-Men II* you will notice that the two sentences are separated by ellipses:

> "When I command in my spirit, the Lord commands with me, for I am one spirit with the Lord." "...Is this my teaching? No! This is the revelation of God in the Bible. It was buried, it was covered for centuries, but by His mercy it has been discovered."

MR. MORGAN: *Is this supposed to be taken from some of Witness Lee's writings?*

DR. MELTON: Both quotes, and there are two quotes instead of one, are taken from a book entitled *How to Meet*.

MR. MORGAN: *Let me show you what has been marked as Exhibit 11, and does that contain the pages from which the quotes were taken?*

DR. MELTON: Yes, it does.

MR. MORGAN: *I'd offer that into evidence, Your Honor.*

JUDGE SEYRANIAN: *May be received.*

MR. MORGAN: *Can you identify for the court where the quotes are that are used?*

DR. MELTON: The quotes are out of order. The second quote appears first in the book beginning with the words:

> Is this my teaching? No! This is the revelation of God in the Bible. It was buried, it was covered for centuries, but by His mercy it has been discovered.

That quote appears on page 94 at the beginning of the last paragraph. The previous quote:

> When I command in my spirit, the Lord commands with me, for I am one spirit with the Lord.

appears on page 97 at the end of the first paragraph in that new section "One with the Lord in Spirit."

MR. MORGAN: *What Mr. Duddy has done then is he has taken one quote and put it ahead of another quote when it wasn't that way in Witness Lee's writings, is that right?*

DR. MELTON: Mr. Duddy has taken two widely separated quotes from the middle of paragraphs and reversed them in order and rammed them together so to speak. The ellipsis implies that one quote follows the other one in fairly close proximity with only irrelevant material being deleted. You would not use an ellipsis to follow a quote several pages later. It might be in the next paragraph but certainly not much further than that.

MR. MORGAN: *The impact created in Mr. Duddy's book is that Witness Lee is saying, "I am speaking for God and I am*

Him speaking, and therefore what I am saying is more important than the Bible." Is that basically the thrust?

DR. MELTON: Right.

MR. MORGAN: *In* How to Meet, *is that what Witness Lee is saying?*

DR. MELTON: Not at all. He is saying something quite different.

MR. MORGAN: *Let's take the one on page 94 of* How to Meet. *What is Witness Lee saying there?*

DR. MELTON: Witness Lee has in the seven or eight pages preceding this been doing a commentary on First Corinthians 12, 13, and 14.

MR. MORGAN: *Those are books of the Bible?*

DR. MELTON: And specific chapters of the books. The material in those chapters concerns the gifts of the Spirit, and in those chapters Paul is talking about the most important gift of the Spirit, which is prophecy, and what he calls the more excellent way, which is love. What Lee has been doing is explicating those two ideas: what is the major gift of the Spirit and what is love. Then he sums up all that he's discussed of Paul and he says, "Is this my teaching?"

The "this" is Paul's teaching on the gift of the Spirit and love. Is this Witness Lee's teaching? No. Paul's teaching is the revelation of God in the Bible. It was buried, it was covered for centuries, but by His mercy it has been discovered.

That is what he is saying. He is not talking about himself at all. He is talking about Paul's discussion of the gifts of the Spirit and love.

MR. MORGAN: *This is just exactly the opposite of what Mr. Duddy is portraying, is that correct?*

DR. MELTON: Right. Witness Lee is putting forth the Bible. He is holding up a Bible and saying, "Believe the Bible."

JUDGE SEYRANIAN: *I am having a little difficulty here. Doctor, maybe I am not reading all of what Duddy says here, but as I understand it, he is simply quoting in context from what is in this book that is written by Witness Lee. Does he someplace before that mention that it is quoted, "Is this my teaching," and it says no. How do you interpret from what appears here in Duddy's book that what he is saying is that this is what Lee is saying?*

DR. MELTON: In Duddy's book he's just been saying that the "Local Church" teaches that Witness Lee is an oracle of God and that Witness Lee agrees with that.

JUDGE SEYRANIAN: *What you are saying is that this context doesn't make reference to chapters twelve, thirteen, and fourteen of Corinthians but rather Witness Lee's teachings?*

DR. MELTON: Right. What it is made to say here is that, "Is it merely Witness Lee's teaching that he is an oracle of God? No, it is the biblical teaching that Witness Lee is an oracle of God." That is what the text says.

MR. MORGAN: *In effect he is saying that Witness Lee is saying that the Bible says, "I am the oracle of God."*

DR. MELTON: Right.

MR. MORGAN: *And that is not at all what Witness Lee was saying, is that right?*

DR. MELTON: Right.

MR. MORGAN: *Now let's go to the quote on page 97. What is Witness Lee saying there?*

DR. MELTON: Okay. Witness Lee is commenting upon a verse in which Paul says, "And unto the married I command yet not I but the Lord." In other words, those are Paul's words.

And he discusses that, and then he closes his sentence by paraphrasing Paul's words, "When I command in my spirit the Lord commands with me for I am one with the Lord."

Now in Duddy's text it is made to appear that the "I" in that sentence is Witness Lee. It is very obvious from reading the text of this that the "I" is Paul and by implication each and every believer who can be like Paul. But it is primarily Paul.

So it is Paul who is saying, "When I command in my spirit, the Lord commands with me," not Witness Lee. And it is made to appear in the text that it is Witness Lee who is claiming authority for himself when he is in fact holding up Paul's authority.

JUDGE SEYRANIAN: *Do you feel, Doctor, that someone of Mr. Duddy's background and his studies and his experiences could have made this as just a mistake or an error, or do you feel that this is a form of intentional misrepresentation? Is this a reasonable misreading of this?*

DR. MELTON: That is the question I started out with and have pondered through this whole thing. The conclusion I have come to is, I don't see how he could have misread it. I quite honestly don't see how. Here is a man, he's got a seminary degree. He concentrated in theology in seminary.

While he doesn't have a doctorate, he certainly is not an unintelligent man. That was shown throughout his deposition. I don't see how he could have done it.

JUDGE SEYRANIAN: *In other words, the way these have been changed is not just a careless or quick reading of it, but it would be something way beyond that?*

DR. MELTON: I thought that at first; I was willing to grant him that point. But after reading his deposition and his pointing out that he had gone over this material in some depth, he didn't just do a quick reading of it.

When I went back over the book again, I realized he could not have constructed the book off of just a quick reading. The book is too sophisticated for that. And this kind of thing happens too many times in Duddy's book. That is the real problem.

MR. MORGAN: *Then as roughly as you like to say it, must you say that it appears to be deliberate?*

DR. MELTON: Yes.

MR. MORGAN: *What is the impact of this kind of a charge against Witness Lee in the eyes of people that will read this book?*

DR. MELTON: Well, had this charge been substantiated, I as an evangelical would no longer be able to fellowship with the "Local Church."

I would not feel comfortable going there and being myself as a Christian and participating in their prayer life and further developing any friendships with members in the church. Witness Lee's books would now take a different position on my bookshelf. They would no longer be considered books that I would read as books written by a fellow Christian. They would now be books that I strictly studied as a scholar.

MR. MORGAN: *Are you saying then that you would want to avoid being around this group and this man?*
DR. MELTON: As a Christian, yes, I could not participate with them anymore.
MR. MORGAN: *Why?*
DR. MELTON: Because as an evangelical I want to worship with people with whom I agree in faith and in thought. I could not honestly sit down and have deep prayer with people who question the authority of the Scriptures.
JUDGE SEYRANIAN: *Would the average person reading this, someone who doesn't have all the degrees and background and experience that you have, do you think they would come to the same conclusion?*
DR. MELTON: Yes, I do. The point that Duddy is making at this point is stated several times rather bluntly. These quotes are merely used to illustrate the charge that is being made. I don't think most people would follow up and see if these quotes really said that. They would just accept what has happened. It's been my experience that most people do not check footnotes.
JUDGE SEYRANIAN: *In your experience and in going through all this material and background and so forth and doing the studying, have you been able to find anything that would give you a reason why Mr. Duddy would have done this? Why would a man like Mr. Duddy do this? Was there anything you found? Was there some break or friction? Was there some problem that occurred between the "Local Church" or Witness Lee?*
DR. MELTON: At one point, early in their life, the Christian World Liberation Front and the "Local Church" had their headquarters in Berkeley right across the street from each other, and there were several incidents of personal confrontations.

There was also an incident in Dallas, in later years, shortly before *The God-Men I* appeared, in which there was some personal confrontation and SCP came out second best.

Every piece of literature I have been able to find on the "Local Church"—Jack Sparks' book *The Mindbenders,* the material the SCP put out, and a number of items derivative of SCP material; and my library is growing all the time—can be traced to that one incident or to the confrontations in Berkeley. I don't know what happened. But that's the best I can make of it.

JUDGE SEYRANIAN: *By the way, we were talking earlier about the stigma in the evangelical movement of being in a cult. Do you remember the time McCarthyism was going on and on about communism? Even though you could prove you were not a communist, you still had the same stigma.*

DR. MELTON: Some of my earliest memories are watching the McCarthy hearings.

JUDGE SEYRANIAN: *Mine too. Do you feel there is that same stigma that once accused there is something that remains?*

DR. MELTON: I think I have put in print on more than one occasion that to call someone a cult is the 1970s equivalent of labeling them a pinko.

MR. MORGAN: *Let me ask you this, sir. First, how many evangelicals would there be in the United States?*

DR. MELTON: Forty million is the usual count.

MR. MORGAN: *As a Christian and as an evangelical, are you concerned about this book?*

DR. MELTON: Very much so.

MR. MORGAN: *In what respect?*

DR. MELTON: As an evangelical I am very much concerned about issues of truth. While I am concerned that, as an evangelical, our position is clearly stated and differentiated from those who disagree with us, I feel that in this case we have defamed some of our own Christian brethren and sisters and have pushed them aside. People that we should be seeing as our friends and allies are being shoved out the door. I am very much concerned about that both as a justice issue and the fact that I as an evangelical and as a Christian have found some communion in meeting with people in the "Local Church."

MR. MORGAN: *Let me go on now to another quote from the Duddy manuscript. You see the word "Scripture." It is the paragraph immediately below it, and we go down just about where it breaks:*

> *Because the epistemological schism affects Lee's view of God's written Word, the Bible assumes a subsidiary position in his sensuous theology. The words of Scripture have meanings, including references to certain facts and events of history, but meaning in general and factuality in particular have less significance for Lee than the personal, subjective experience of Christ in the human spirit. This experience can be opened up to us through reading the Bible, but it occurs through a process of spiritual osmosis which has nothing to do with understanding what we read. The written Word is a shadow, not a reality. A higher spiritual Word exists behind the rational meaning of the written Word. The written Word acts like an erratic compass rather than a definitive guide to reality. Commenting on Romans 2:29 and 7:6, where Paul writes that Christians are released from the penalty of the law (the letter), Lee writes: "Now we know what the word 'letter' here refers to—it is the written Bible. Today we must serve the living Lord with newness in the spirit, not according to the oldness of the written Bible. Everyone must admit that the word 'letter' in these passages refers to the written Scriptures. There can be no argument."*

Can you tell the court what significance that has to a reader of this type of material?

DR. MELTON: Well, the significance of this is to suggest that Lee, while he uses the Bible, places it in a secondary position, that the Bible is a useful tool to get something else that is more important.

MR. MORGAN: *How significant is that in the evangelical religion?*

DR. MELTON: Well, the Bible's our authority, and certainly there is a place for saying that the Bible is to help us gain faith in Jesus Christ, but we would never degrade the Bible. We would never downplay its significance. It is always there. It is not merely a tool to get somewhere else.

MR. MORGAN: *Then is this part of the book telling the readers that Witness Lee is downgrading the Bible?*

DR. MELTON: It is telling them, the reader, and it says it in very specific terms in Duddy's text, that Lee downgrades the authority of Scripture.

MR. MORGAN: *What effect would that have on Witness Lee and members of the "Local Church" in the evangelical community?*

DR. MELTON: It would make them anathema.

MR. MORGAN: *Does that mean they are not wanted?*

DR. MELTON: Very much so.

MR. MORGAN: *Again, does Mr. Duddy purportedly rely on certain quotes from Witness Lee in this regard?*

DR. MELTON: Yes, in this particular regard the quote comes out of his book *Christ vs. Religion.*

[*Christ vs. Religion* by Witness Lee, marked for identification as plaintiff's Exhibit 12.]

MR. MORGAN: *Showing you what's been marked as Exhibit 12, can you identify what that is?*

DR. MELTON: These are some pages from Witness Lee's book, *Christ vs. Religion.* The two quotes at the end of the paragraph under discussion were taken from two sentences on pages 152 and 153.

MR. MORGAN: *I will offer that into evidence as Exhibit 12, Your Honor.*

JUDGE SEYRANIAN: *May be admitted.*

MR. MORGAN: *First let me talk a bit about that title. That sounds kind of blasphemous,* Christ vs. Religion. *What does that mean?*

DR. MELTON: It means that in Witness Lee's view, human beings make up religion. All human beings are religious, and they will make up things to do and to be and believe and follow which are religious and that Christ as the living presence of God breaks through that manmade religion and becomes a living reality to the Christian. Faith in Christ stands over against manmade religion.

MR. MORGAN: *In manmade religion, are we talking about practices and temples?*

DR. MELTON: We are talking about codes of law and practice. We are talking about ritual. We are talking about church structures, particularly bishops and priests. We are talking about all the things that people do to be religious.

MR. MORGAN: *Is there something wrong about saying that?*

DR. MELTON: I don't think so. It has been a fairly popular idea in twentieth century theology. A number of twentieth century theologians, some evangelical, some not so, have proposed that idea. Karl Barth is probably the most famous theologian that has written a massive volume on the same theme.

MR. MORGAN: *It is not something that is totally new or way out or anything; it is something that's already been expressed. Is that right?*

DR. MELTON: Yes.

MR. MORGAN: *Let's go to the quotes in* Christ vs. Religion. *Let's take the first one on page 152:*

> *Romans 7:6 says, "But now we have been discharged from the law, having died to that wherein we were held; so that we serve in newness of the spirit, and not in oldness of the letter." Now we know what the word "letter" here refers to–it is the written Bible. Today we must serve the living Lord with newness in the spirit, not according to the oldness of the written Bible. I can say this boldly, because I am a little follower of this most bold one, the Apostle Paul. Now we serve not according to the oldness of the written code, the written Bible, but according to the newness of the spirit. Why? Because in the spirit is Christ, while in the written code is religion. This is Christ versus religion.*
>
> *What is it to be religious? To be religious is simply to be sound, scriptural, and fundamental, yet without the presence of Christ. If we lack His presence, regardless of how scriptural we are, we are simply religious. Paul in these two verses of Romans laid a solid foundation for Christ versus religion. Today our service, our work, and even our life must be altogether in the spirit, not merely according to the letters of the written Bible. I know that when I say this I run a risk. I will be charged with the heresy of turning people away from the Bible. But I simply refer you to these two passages of Scripture, Romans 2:29 and Romans 7:6. Everyone must admit that the word "letter" in these passages refers to the written Scriptures. There can be no argument. Christ is versus religion; Christ is versus the written code. We may have the right quotation from the written code, yet miss Christ, just as the Pharisees and scribes in ancient times. We must be alert not to pay that much attention to the written code. If we do, it is altogether possible and extremely probable that we will miss*

Christ. The only way of safety is to behold "with unveiled face the glory of the Lord" (II Cor. 3:18).

Tell the court what Witness Lee is saying there.

DR. MELTON: Witness Lee is discussing a particular point of religion, namely the Old Testament codification of the law. We think of the Old Testament law as being the Ten Commandments. In actuality, it covers a couple of books of the Bible and is a very detailed presentation of the law. And then the Jewish continuance of the codification in the Talmud and in their writings.

What he is talking about here is the attempt to codify religion into a written code, and he is using this as an example. The Old Testament law, that is what he is discussing at this point.

MR. MORGAN: *What does he say there?*

DR. MELTON: He is saying that the Old Testament written code has been set over against Christ, that Christ has put it behind us and is opposed to it.

MR. MORGAN: *When he says, "Now we know what the word 'letter' here refers to—it is the written Bible," what is he talking about there?*

DR. MELTON: Well, I suspect if I could see a movie of this that what Witness Lee is doing is he is holding up a Bible in his hand, and he is referring to the front of it or to the Old Testament portion of it and saying, this becomes a written code for us, and we must not let the written code get in the way of our faith in Jesus Christ. That is simply, pretty much what he is saying.

MR. MORGAN: *Is that saying that the Bible takes a secondary or inferior position?*

DR. MELTON: No, it is saying something that evangelical dispensational theology and what most of Christian theology has said through the years. It agrees with Paul. The law had its purpose. It was a schoolmaster. It led us to Christ, and Christ nailed it to the cross, and we are now Christians, and we do not follow that Old Testament code anymore. It is something that Christ broke through.

MR. MORGAN: *When you say you don't follow it, are you saying you ignore it?*

DR. MELTON: The greater part of it, yes.

JUDGE SEYRANIAN: *Is it supplemented by the New Testament?*

DR. MELTON: No. The following of the greater part of the Old Testament code has simply been set aside. Remembering that there is a small section of it which we call the Ten Commandments, that is generally considered to be the moral code which he treats elsewhere, but the greater part of it has to do with ritual performance, the keeping of feasts, what food you can eat. That all has been set aside. That was all religion, and that is what Witness Lee is saying.

MR. MORGAN: *Just so we don't leave this dangling, what does Witness Lee say about the Ten Commandments?*

DR. MELTON: He says the Ten Commandments are God's immutable laws, that they are for all times and all places, and that they must be followed.

JUDGE SEYRANIAN: *The evangelical movement, do they believe in both the New Testament and the Old Testament?*

DR. MELTON: Both.

JUDGE SEYRANIAN: *When you refer to the Bible you are referring to the combination of the Old and the New Testament.*

DR. MELTON: Right.

MR. MORGAN: *Now let's go down to the next one at the bottom of the page which says:*

> Everyone must admit that the word "letter" in these passages refers to the written Scriptures. There can be no argument.

Again, what is Lee saying there?

DR. MELTON: He is making the same point over again that we do not follow the letter of the law. The letter of the law is found in the Old Testament. Paul didn't have a New Testament, so when Paul refers to the written Scriptures, he is referring to the Old Testament. That is where the rules and regulations about ritual and diet are found.

MR. MORGAN: *You have told us that Duddy has used these*

two quotes to say that Witness Lee put the Bible in a secondary or inferior position, is that right?
DR. MELTON: That's right.
MR. MORGAN: *Those quotes don't say that, do they?*
DR. MELTON: No.
MR. MORGAN: *They say just the opposite again, don't they?*
DR. MELTON: Yes.
MR. MORGAN: *Again, is this something that an individual like Mr. Duddy, assuming he read the materials of Witness Lee that he says, that he could ever make such a statement?*
DR. MELTON: This one is somewhat harder than the others. The quotes here are very strong and especially taken out by themselves are very strong. I could see where Mr. Duddy could have read the book, and those quotes could have jumped out at him. But, no, Mr. Duddy is an intelligent, trained person. He should have understood how Witness Lee is using the material here and the analogy that he is making.

It is obvious that Witness Lee is speaking hyperbolically, that he is not stopping to say "what I mean" or the Scriptures in Leviticus and Numbers and these specific points. He is just saying the Scriptures. That is a hyperbole, but it is obvious from the context what he is doing.
MR. MORGAN: *And if one were to read the rest of his writings, is it obvious that Witness Lee hasn't said that?*
DR. MELTON: Certainly it is. You read Witness Lee's writings over and over and over again, and Duddy would have encountered these facts in his vast reading. Witness Lee holds up the Bible, the written Bible, the written word, and tells people that it is to be believed and to be studied and to be learned, and how Duddy could have missed those; he doesn't quote any of those passages, but they are scattered so much through his writings.
JUDGE SEYRANIAN: *Let me see if I understand what you are saying. Are you saying that in Duddy's word he is saying that Witness Lee is almost putting the Bible aside, whereas Witness Lee in his writings is saying that the letter is reference to the Old Testament which we put aside and look to the New Testament?*

DR. MELTON: No, that is not what he is saying. What Witness Lee is saying is that there is a portion of the Old Testament which is merely the codification of the law that God gave to the Jews at a specific time and place. That code, that written code, has been put aside. That is all Lee is saying.

JUDGE SEYRANIAN: *But Duddy says his reference is to the entire Bible, the New Testament as well?*

DR. MELTON: The context with which it appears in Duddy is a reference to the entire Scripture, and it is not just putting aside—it is downgrading all of Scripture.

MR. MORGAN: *Then does Mr. Duddy work this ultimately into his book to create an idea that because of this Witness Lee somehow encourages immorality?*

DR. MELTON: That is where this is leading. If the Bible and particularly the legal parts of the Bible have been put aside, then they no longer have to be followed. Duddy has created the image that Witness Lee is teaching a spiritualized theology, where the only thing that is important is your relationship spiritually to God and that the moral code has been set aside so that you are free to do various immoral things.

In actual fact, over and over again in his writings, Lee says that the Ten Commandments are for all times and all places and all people, and he has one rather humorous item where he is talking about prayer and seeking personal guidance through prayer. He says you don't go to God and pray, "God, should I steal" and seek guidance on that matter.

He says, "No, the law has been given; it says don't steal. That is it. You don't even ask God about that because God has already spoken on that issue."

In another place where he is discussing Christ fulfilling the law, he says, "Why did the Ten Commandments have to be fulfilled in Christ? He said because they were incomplete. The Ten Commandments said don't murder. That means don't murder. It didn't say anything about anger. You can get angry, and Moses didn't have anything against you. Christ said now you can't even get angry."

That is law. You've got to follow that. It's for all times, all places, all people.

MR. MORGAN: *Let me ask you to turn to another quote from* The God-Men, *where it says:*

> Consistently, Lee's counsel steers parishioners away from biblical ethic regarding behavior and teachings which encourage responsibility and affirmative action. Paul's counsel to Timothy as cited earlier (II Timothy 3:16-17) heralds Scripture as being useful for "teaching, rebuking, correcting and training in righteousness"—a counsel which lies dormant in Lee's sensuous theology.

Again, that is the end of the part I am quoting. Is this again where Mr. Duddy is conveying the idea that Witness Lee's teachings are leading towards immorality?

DR. MELTON: That is the exact point he is making. He is saying that Lee discounts following moral law, and therefore breaking moral law is okay for a member of the "Local Church." That is just totally the opposite of what Lee consistently teaches through his books.

MR. MORGAN: *We have on the board here pages 150 and 155 from* Christ vs. Religion. *Witness Lee says:*

> I do have scriptural ground to say that what we need is something in the spirit, not anything merely in the letter according to the written Scriptures. Who can argue? Please do not misunderstand me: I am not saying, nor have I ever said, that we should not care for the Scriptures. [page 150]

> Some may charge us with being too liberal; they may call us "liberal Christians." But be careful: this term "liberal Christian" refers to the modernists who do not believe that the Bible is the divine revelation, nor that Jesus Christ is the Son of God, who accomplished redemption, was resurrected, and ascended to the heavens. They are the liberal ones; we are not. We would die for the Bible. We believe that the Bible is God's divine Word, and we believe that our Lord Jesus is the very God incarnated to be a man, who died on the cross for our sins, and was resurrected physically, spiritually, and literally. [page 155]

He is saying that the Scriptures are up there, is that right?

DR. MELTON: Right. At this point he is discussing, as he

discusses throughout the Scripture, that there is the problem of people who know Scripture from a rather secular, studious point of view but have never inculcated in their lives the substance of what Scripture is talking about.

It is like a person who could quote the thirteenth chapter of Corinthians about love but who doesn't know how to love; they've never experienced love. They know the letter of Scripture, but they don't understand what it is all about. He is saying we not only must know that letter of Scripture, but we must experience it and make it a part of our lives. That is what he is getting to.

MR. MORGAN: *Now that is on page 150 which is from* Christ vs. Religion, *so that is just a matter of two pages before the part that Mr. Duddy took out of the quote is that right?*

DR. MELTON: That's right.

MR. MORGAN: *So Mr. Duddy had to have read right from the start what Witness Lee was saying?*

DR. MELTON: That's right.

MR. MORGAN: *Does that indicate to you that in this instance it was deliberate?*

DR. MELTON: It indicates it to me. The second quote you have up there indicates it a lot more, because in the second quote he is talking about people who are liberal Christians and he specifically says that liberal Christians are people who do not believe in the revelation of the Bible as God's Word. We are not that. We would die for the Bible. That is such a clear and blatant statement of his position that even if Duddy was a little sleepy when he got to page 150, there is no way to miss the implication on page 155.

MR. MORGAN: *And that is when he said he would die for the Bible.*

DR. MELTON: Right.

MR. MORGAN: *Let me go to another quote of Duddy's:*

> Biblically, God manifests perfect holiness because he is self-consistent, not because he obeys an extraneous, higher law. Lee reasons that because Christians, too, are divine, they should not be bound by external moral laws.

Again, what is that saying?

DR. MELTON: It is saying that you don't have to follow the Ten Commandments. You don't have to follow the Sermon on the Mount.

MR. MORGAN: *That is entirely contrary to what Witness Lee says, is that right?*

DR. MELTON: Exactly.

MR. MORGAN: *In that instance he says, "...because Christians, too, are divine." What is the significance of that?*

DR. MELTON: This has to do with the doctrine of God that the "Local Church" uses, their particular use of a language around the term *mingling*. It has been Duddy's interpretation that the use of that language implies that once one becomes a member of the "Local Church," it is Lee's conception that they mingle with God in such a way that they become something different than human, that they are now a kind of human-divine hybrid. That is the import of the name of the book, *The God-Men;* they are a different species because they have mingled with the divine. What he is saying here is that because they are this different species that is why they have been released from the law.

MR. MORGAN: *Are you saying then that the title of the book, The God-Men, is implying to the readers that the people of the "Local Church" are in fact a different form of species because of their belief?*

DR. MELTON: Yes, that is the implication of the title.

MR. MORGAN: *All right. Did you come across some evidence of what Mr. Duddy did as far as this divine concept in altering a diagram of Witness Lee's?*

DR. MELTON: The main place that this happens, again it relates to biblical authority and law. It has to do with Lee's book *Christ and the Church Revealed and Typified in the Psalms*. There is a diagram in there that appears around page 41 or 42 in Duddy's book.

MR. MORGAN: *Let's mark this as Exhibit 13 and ask you if you can identify what that is.*

DR. MELTON: Exhibit 13 is two pages, pages 40 and 41 from Witness Lee's book *Christ and the Church Revealed and*

Typified in the Psalms, and the book itself is a commentary on the book of Psalms.

MR. MORGAN: *Is that referred to by Mr. Duddy in his book?*

DR. MELTON: Yes, it is. And in the middle of page 40 there is a diagram which Duddy purports to reproduce in his book.

MR. MORGAN: *I will offer that into evidence as Exhibit 13.*

JUDGE SEYRANIAN: *May be accepted.*

EXHIBIT 13

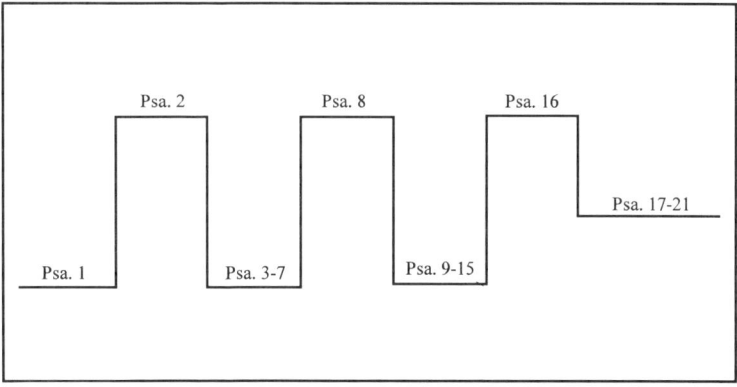

Christ and the Church Revealed and Typified in the Psalms
by Witness Lee

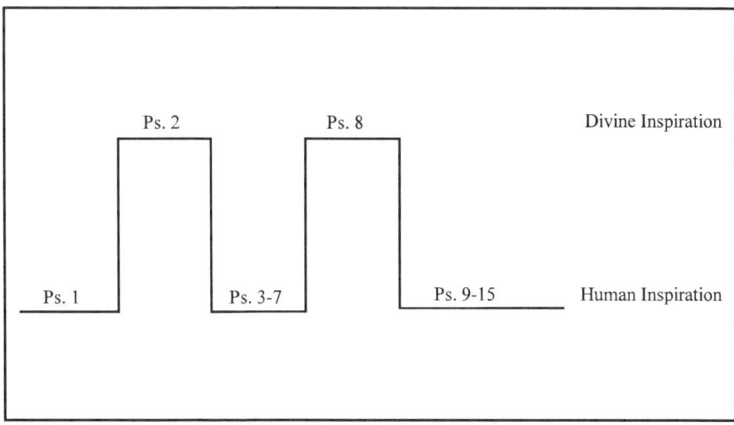

THE GOD-MEN: An Inquiry into Witness Lee & the Local Church
by Neil Duddy & the SCP

MR. MORGAN: *First, Doctor, can you tell us what the diagram in Witness Lee's writing is supposed to indicate?*

DR. MELTON: Witness Lee divides the Psalms into two classes. First, those that primarily refer to upholding and celebrating the Old Testament law and God's covenant with Israel. A second set of Psalms primarily foreshadow and look toward the coming of Christ, and what Lee does is to suggest that the Psalms that look toward Christ are of a higher quality. He uses the term *higher.* How would we describe it? They are of more spiritual import to the Christian today than those which celebrate the law.

MR. MORGAN: *Let me do this. Let me hold up a copy of* Christ and the Church Revealed and Typified in the Psalms *and ask you to look at page 40, Doctor. Now we have, right down at the bottom it says Psalm 1, then up at the top it is Psalm 2 and Psalms 3 to 7, Psalm 8, Psalms 9 to 15, Psalm 16, and then Psalms 17 to 21.*

DR. MELTON: Right.

MR. MORGAN: *Is there some significance there between Psalm 1 and Psalm 2?*

DR. MELTON: Yes.

MR. MORGAN: *And what is the significance?*

DR. MELTON: Psalm 1 and Psalms 3 to 7 are on the lower level. They are Psalms which are seen as celebrating the law and the Old Testament. The Psalms on the higher level are those that are celebrating the coming of Christ and the church.

MR. MORGAN: *Duddy on page 42 of* The God-Men II *apparently attempts to create that, is that correct?*

DR. MELTON: He claims that he's reproduced that diagram.

MR. MORGAN: *Just by looking at it we can see it is not the same, is that right?*

DR. MELTON: Right. He's deleted material in the diagram.

MR. MORGAN: *First, what is the significance of the deletion of material?*

DR. MELTON: The most significant thing is it is simply changed. He's claimed he's reproduced the diagram and he hasn't.

MR. MORGAN: *In addition, has he added something to it?*

DR. MELTON: He's added two lines to it.

MR. MORGAN: *What are they?*

DR. MELTON: If I remember correctly, "Divine Inspiration" and "Human Inspiration."

MR. MORGAN: *They are off to the side, is that right?*

DR. MELTON: Yes.

MR. MORGAN: *What is the significance of adding those words there?*

DR. MELTON: The significance is that Duddy is telling the reader that some Psalms are merely humanly inspired, and some Psalms are divinely inspired. Therefore, there are some parts of the Bible which we don't have to pay attention to because they are merely human inspiration; and there are some Psalms that are divinely inspired, and those we should pay attention to.

MR. MORGAN: *Is Mr. Duddy representing that Witness Lee says that?*

DR. MELTON: Yes, and by putting those words in the diagram, he is representing to the reader that Lee has those words either in the diagram or at least in the text of the chapter.

MR. MORGAN: *Does Witness Lee have those words in there?*

DR. MELTON: He not only does not have those words; he has nothing that even remotely resembles those concepts.

JUDGE SEYRANIAN: *I thought you said that Witness Lee does say that the ones on the upper level are more spiritual. They have more of a spiritual import than the ones on the lower level and that the lower level are more like the Old Testament.*

DR. MELTON: That is right, but they are no less godly inspired. Lee is a dispensationalist, and dispensational theology says that God has acted at different periods of time in an evermore inclusive sense.

In other words, revelation has been added to through time, and dispensationalists would say that the revelation of Christ is more universal and supersedes the revelation of the law. But the revelation of the law is no less divinely inspired. God gave the law, God made the covenant with Israel, and God led Israel.

What a dispensationalist would say is that Christ's

revelation supersedes that revelation, and that is what Lee is saying. It is not that the law is humanly inspired, is a human product. It is of God; it is divine just as the New Testament is, but it has been superseded.

JUDGE SEYRANIAN: *Is Lee saying that, or is he saying that these Psalms, that it had on the lower level, where Duddy says human inspiration, are a human translation of those Psalms?*

DR. MELTON: What Duddy is saying is that it is inspired out of human experience, not out of God's experience, and, therefore, that part of the Bible is to be discounted and no attention paid to it because it is merely of human inspiration. An evangelical would say the entire Scripture is inspired by God.

JUDGE SEYRANIAN: *Duddy seems to infer that it is Lee's teaching that Christ is supreme even over above the written text. If you take the Bible up here, and you take Christ up here, Christ has to be above the Bible because it is His teachings. What he is saying, at least this is what he ascribes to Witness Lee, is that sometimes it is not what is written but it is what Christ's teachings are that is the most important. Do you get that feeling?*

DR. MELTON: Yes. I get that feeling.

JUDGE SEYRANIAN: *Is that what Witness Lee says?*

DR. MELTON: No. Witness Lee would say that the most important thing in life is our faith and relationship for saving faith with God. The Bible is integral to that experience because it is the Bible that is the way we learn about that experience and make our connection. It is not a mere intermediary between us and God, but it is integral to that, and it is the entire Scripture that was given to us by God.

JUDGE SEYRANIAN: *There is someplace I read in here that Witness Lee says it is not the man who holds the Bible up that is important if he doesn't believe in the living Christ.*

DR. MELTON: That's right.

JUDGE SEYRANIAN: *So it is not all important just simply holding the Bible in your hand, but it is believing in the teachings of the living Christ. Isn't that what Lee teaches?*

DR. MELTON: That is exactly what Lee and evangelicals teach, totally. As I said before, it is important that we know the thirteenth chapter of Corinthians about Paul's teachings on love. It is equally important that we be loving people.

JUDGE SEYRANIAN: *What is the feeling of the evangelical if you get a person who quotes the Bible, holds the Bible in their hands, but doesn't practice what it says?*

DR. MELTON: They would tend to look down upon that person.

JUDGE SEYRANIAN: *It is not the holding of the Bible or being able to quote it or being familiar with it, but it is living it, isn't it? Or do they believe in it?*

DR. MELTON: Living the Scriptures is one sign that you really believe it. Hypocrisy, of course, is a great sin in most religions: to say "I believe it" and go out and do the exact opposite.

This is one of the things that amazes me about this particular set of charges about Lee. Here is a man who has spent his entire adult life getting up in front of people and teaching on the Bible.

If he did not believe the Bible was the written word of God, he would be one of the most unique men in history. I have never heard of anyone who has spent his entire life doing biblical exposition who didn't believe that the Bible was the most important thing going. That is one of those things that amazes me.

MR. MORGAN: *Doctor, there is nothing in Witness Lee's writings or words upon which Mr. Duddy could say that Witness Lee is placing the Bible in a lesser position, is there?*

DR. MELTON: No, I don't think so. I have read twenty or so of his books, and I have not found anything that implies remotely that he degrades the Bible.

MR. MORGAN: *Just to the opposite, he is saying things such as, "We would die for the Bible," is that right?*

DR. MELTON: Yes. It is also the church's official position in their statement of faith, which Mr. Duddy had access to. The very first statement is, "We believe that the Holy Bible is the complete divine revelation verbally inspired by the Holy Spirit."

JUDGE SEYRANIAN: *Is it your feeling that an average person, not one educated like you, the average person reading Duddy's book would get the idea that Witness Lee downgrades the Bible?*
DR. MELTON: Duddy says it over and over so many times, I don't see how it could escape even the most ignorant of readers.
MR. MORGAN: *And that would go in here where Mr. Duddy is purporting to say or is saying that Witness Lee says the Bible is not inspired, am I right?*
DR. MELTON: Right.
MR. MORGAN: *Let's move on, then. You will see the words, "Charles Finney and Asa Mahan" and then Mr. Duddy says,*

> Evidently, Lee incorporates moral pygmyism in his discussion on ethics. Moral pygmies are believers whose standard of conduct plunges far below the ethical code of the law, while remaining oblivious to the disparity.

First, what is that saying to the reader?
DR. MELTON: It is saying that Witness Lee's presentations of moral standards are stone age: moral pygmies, people who haven't grown up, pre-civilized, have not yet heard the law.
MR. MORGAN: *And is it saying, then, that these people can do immoral acts and actually be oblivious to the fact that they are committing immoral acts?*
DR. MELTON: They would have no conscience about them. Certainly, yes.
MR. MORGAN: *Is there anything in Witness Lee's teachings that indicates that?*
DR. MELTON: Not at all.
MR. MORGAN: *Is there anything that indicates to the contrary?*
DR. MELTON: There are numerous quotes. The one you have from *The Economy of God* is just one of many in which, as we said earlier, the law, the Ten Commandments, is a set of fixed rules which cannot be changed. That is the quote concerning prayer. Don't pray for guidance and of whether or not the Ten Commandments still hold for you.
MR. MORGAN: *Would you agree that the term* moral pygmy, *as used here, is a pejorative term, a damaging term?*

DR. MELTON: Oh, very much so.

MR. MORGAN: *Again, would you agree that in this instance Neil Duddy is deliberately distorting Witness Lee's teachings?*

DR. MELTON: He is not only distorting Witness Lee's teachings; he is distorting Benjamin Warfield's teachings too.

MR. MORGAN: *Who is Benjamin Warfield?*

DR. MELTON: Benjamin Warfield is a very conservative, outstanding, Presbyterian theologian from the early part of this century. He's one of the people strongly referred to at the seminary where Mr. Duddy attended in Philadelphia.

MR. MORGAN: *What part does Mr. Warfield play in this citation?*

DR. MELTON: Mr. Warfield wrote a book on sanctification in which he opposed the Presbyterian ideals of sanctification against those of the Methodists and the Holiness people.

MR. MORGAN: *The word* sanctification, *what does that mean?*

DR. MELTON: You really want to get into that?

JUDGE SEYRANIAN: *That may take us a while.*

MR. MORGAN: *Can you give it to me in simple language?*

DR. MELTON: Sanctification means holy. How is the Christian made holy? How is he sanctified? Presbyterians essentially say, "In this life one is made holy only by faith. One becomes truly holy in the next life." The Holiness and Methodists said, "No, one can become holy in this life."

Asa Mahan and Charles Finney were two Congregationalists who were strongly affected by Methodist doctrine and became leaders in the Holiness movement. What Warfield was doing was opposing these ideas.

The Methodists had accused the Presbyterians of antinomianism, that is, being people who do not follow the law. It was part of the particular term they had picked out: "To be a Presbyterian is to be an anti-nomian, without the law."

What Warfield is doing is returning kind for kind saying, "To be a member of the Holiness movement and teach their view of sanctification is to be a moral pygmy." Moral pygmyism refers to their interpretation of the doctrine of sanctification as being "something that we can work towards rather than something God has to give us." That is what Warfield is saying about the Holiness doctrine.

MR. MORGAN: *Are you saying that Mr. Duddy even made up the definition of moral pygmyism here?*
DR. MELTON: He certainly changed it from that which Warfield had used. Warfield uses the term in a massive theological tome which only ten people have ever read. It is buried in the middle of it. It is one of his minor words, and he is using it as part of a scholarly theological polemic about people who aren't alive anymore.
MR. MORGAN: *Let me ask you, would Mr. Finney and Mr. Mahan actually be moral pygmies according to Duddy's definition?*
DR. MELTON: I would not think so. It should be pointed out that Warfield did not accuse either Mahan or Finney of immorality or of being less than staunch, full members of the Christian community. By moral pygmies he is accusing them of theological defect in their doctrine of sanctification.

Asa Mahan and Charles Finney are two of the finest Christians this country ever produced. Finney wrote the first, the original, systematic theology of the Protestant church after the American Revolution.

Mahan and Finney were the leaders of Oberlin Theological School, which was the bedrock of the abolitionist movement. During the years they were there, it was about the only place a black man could get a theological education or a woman a college education. They developed a whole theology about the moral government of God. They were some of the people who made American theology with its imprint of integrating moral categories into political life. Woodrow Wilson's idea of waiting to get into World War I until he had a moral reason comes out of Finney's ideal.

No, Warfield was not accusing them of immorality or of moral pygmyism in the sense of doing immoral things or teaching immoral things. He was accusing them of a defect in the doctrine of sanctification.
MR. MORGAN: *Again, without belaboring it, to charge that Witness Lee is teaching people so that they can be immoral and be oblivious to it will obviously have a devastating effect on Witness Lee and the "Local Church," won't it?*
DR. MELTON: To say the least. His reputation in the church

would be damaged beyond measure, but even his public reputation outside the church. Here is a religious leader teaching people to be immoral or teaching you can be immoral.

MR. MORGAN: *I want to go to another quote from* The God-Men:

> Second, the Anaheim official pointed out that other Christian churches are riddled with similar improprieties and transgressions. Whereas the Christian community has witnessed moments of division and immorality among its members, characteristically biblical discipline has been exercised to exhort such members to repentance. Within the Local Church, however, sensuous theology tends to enhance this type of social interaction because Scripture is relegated to a non-valued position and is not revered as the voice of authority that traditional propositional theology assigns it.

The words sensual theology, *what is that?*

DR. MELTON: It is a fairly complicated concept that Duddy developed. It is his description of Witness Lee's theology. It carries several imports to it, among them being that one's experience of the divine life is more important than the teachings of Scripture. Secondly, it carries with it the idea that the metaphors that one uses to describe the Christian life are taken from sense experience. They are sensuous. Those are the basic imports of the concept.

MR. MORGAN: *Does Witness Lee teach that?*

DR. MELTON: He certainly draws some metaphors from sensual experience. In that way he is following some traditional theological lines. If Duddy had been aware of his own tradition a little more, he might have known of Jonathan Edwards' sermon in which he compares the Christian life to the taste of honey for the first time, a very sensual concept.

I cannot explain faith to you. It is like trying to explain what honey tastes like if you have never tasted honey. So in that sense Duddy complains about something that Lee is doing that the best of theologians have always done. On the other hand, Lee does emphasize the experience of Christian life, but he does not do it in such a way that it downgrades the Scripture or puts aside scriptural authority. As a matter of fact, he does it because of scriptural authority. The Scripture does emphasize that we must live the Christian life and that we must experience the Holy Spirit in our lives and in our communal life. That is not downgrading Scripture as Duddy implies. It is living Scripture.

MR. MORGAN: *Continuing on that same page, Duddy says:*

> *Not only is the Local Church unwilling to exercise discipline, but, by intrinsic theological design, its ability to do so is foundationally inadequate because authority rests in conscious sensations from the Spirit-spirit whose voices may be many and varied.*

What is he saying there?

DR. MELTON: He is saying a couple of things.

Number one, he is saying, Forget for a moment that I said Witness Lee runs the church with an iron hand and that he controls everybody and manipulates everybody, because what really is happening is there is chaos in the "Local Church," and they are all doing their own thing because they are spirit-led. So he is basically contradicting his own self.

But the point he is trying to make here is that Witness Lee has built a theology, and the "Local Church" has accepted a theology where individual spirit guidance is the way you make decisions rather than applying to the Scripture for guidance.

MR. MORGAN: *Is he saying that you really don't realize that you are approving immoral acts, as an example?*

DR. MELTON: That's right. You are approving acts that you have been taught in childhood were immoral because everybody is a convert. But now they no longer appear immoral to you because you have gotten the word from inside yourself and from your spirit that what you want to do is okay.

EDITOR'S NOTE: *Dr. Melton was asked about the following incident only to establish that a reader would falsely understand it as a consequence of Witness Lee's teaching.*

Other witnesses at the trial testified, proving the falsity of the alleged incident. See Dr. Saliba, page 97.

MR. MORGAN: *Now this is following a story about a child rape, is it not?*

DR. MELTON: As best as I remember, it is.

MR. MORGAN: *So in effect, then, Mr. Duddy is saying that Witness Lee's teaching in this regard bears some responsibility for this child rape, is that correct?*

DR. MELTON: It would free someone to do immoral things without a guilty conscience.

MR. MORGAN: *Isn't he also saying that the people in the church aren't even prepared to discipline one for that because they don't accept it as wrong?*

DR. MELTON: That's right.

MR. MORGAN: *And that's totally false as far as Witness Lee and the "Local Church," is that right?*

DR. MELTON: Totally false.

MR. MORGAN: *Again, in your opinion, making this kind of a charge against Witness Lee and the "Local Church," was this something that had to have been deliberate?*

DR. MELTON: Certainly the charge was deliberate. To connect the charge with these teachings that ignore what Witness Lee has said about the necessity of members following the law, had to be either deliberate or some kind of reckless disregard of what Lee had obviously said.

MR. MORGAN: *Doctor, throughout these publications, are there allegations by Mr. Duddy and SCP of some form of psychological damage to the members of the "Local Church"?*

DR. MELTON: Yes, there is. In particular, there is a charge that members of the "Local Church" have a loss of mental acuity.

MR. MORGAN: *And what in the world is mental acuity?*

DR. MELTON: They have a loss of ability to deal rationally with what most of us think of as the real world.

MR. MORGAN: *In your interrelation with the members, have you found anything of that sort?*

DR. MELTON: Not at all.

MR. MORGAN: *Can you tell the court what you have seen in Witness Lee's writings regarding education?*

DR. MELTON: There is in several places a strong admonition of the members to use and develop their minds. In one place in particular he points out to the younger members of the church that we are no longer living in Israel, we are not farmers, and he equates going to college as planting a crop and getting a degree as harvesting it. He admonishes all of them to go to college and to get their degree.

MR. MORGAN: *I am going to ask you to look at another Duddy quote, where it says:*

> Public humiliation occurs sporadically and for varying reasons. One case in point was the arrangement by Lee to have an elder denounce the Rapoports before an audience of 1,000 plus Anaheim parishioners. The family was cited for deserting the faith, analogous to Hymenaeus and Alexander, who "suffered shipwreck in regard to their faith" (I Timothy 1:19, 20).

Then Duddy goes on and talks about another person, and when we get over to this page, he says:

> Rapoport confirmed that this fear of being "singled out," or the actual event itself, has contributed to the emotional breakdowns of a disconcertingly high number of Anaheim church members, necessitating their hospitalization in psychiatric wards.

In your study of the church, have you seen any evidence of that?

DR. MELTON: No.

MR. MORGAN: *Let me ask you, in either the reading of Witness Lee's writings or looking at the videotapes, is there anything that you see there that would be a singling out or an ostracizing that would cause people to be hospitalized in psychiatric wards?*

DR. MELTON: Nothing.

MR. MORGAN: *Was there a cult leader who became known for singling out and ostracizing people and in effect harming them psychologically?*

DR. MELTON: There have been several. Of course, the most famous one is Jim Jones.

MR. MORGAN: *Let me ask you again, and it may be belaboring the issue. What impact does that kind of language have upon the Christian community when there are writings saying that a man is creating this psychological damage to people?*

DR. MELTON: Well, the main impact concerns a family member who might join, and it raises a specter of fear. For example, if my daughter became a member of the "Local Church," and I believed this, I would be fearful of her health and welfare.

MR. MORGAN: *Is this the sort of thing that we are reading about in the newspapers where families are trying to get their children out of various groups and are using deprogramming?*

DR. MELTON: Deprogramming is certainly one of the things that some parents who have developed this kind of fear have used against various groups.

MR. MORGAN: *Let me ask another question now. How are Witness Lee and the "Local Church" able to counter this charge?*

DR. MELTON: It's almost impossible. It's like charging them with witchcraft. You can deny it, but it is such a nebulous thing, and it is very difficult to deal with, especially with the press.

JUDGE SEYRANIAN: *I have a question, Doctor. I was going to ask you it earlier. Trying to get back again to understand what you did, because you are not a regular member of this church. I understand you read a lot of the writings of Witness Lee and that early in 1970 you attended some of the "Local Church's" meetings. About how many would this have been at that time that you attended?*

DR. MELTON: It was in the mid-seventies that I actually attended the meetings. I attended ten or twelve over a period of a couple of years.

JUDGE SEYRANIAN: *You weren't a real active participant, and you'd come and go, I take it?*

DR. MELTON: Right.

JUDGE SEYRANIAN: *Obviously a good member of the "Local Church" would attend more than ten or twelve in two years, right?*

DR. MELTON: Right.

JUDGE SEYRANIAN: *You were retained to do some checking to see the truth or untruth of the statements that were in this book,* The God-Men, *and in that regard you then went back to the "Local Church," didn't you?*
DR. MELTON: Yes.
JUDGE SEYRANIAN: *About how many more meetings did you attend?*
DR. MELTON: I attended three or four more in Chicago and three or four more in Southern California.
JUDGE SEYRANIAN: *What else did you do in your investigative processes? Obviously you compared the writings. Did you talk to any regular members?*
DR. MELTON: Oh, yes. That's one of the things I made my original evaluation on, because my original visits to the church in the mid-seventies had occurred just as the deprogramming, brainwashing scare had come along. In my first visits I just went as a person off the street; I did not identify myself as anyone special.

I sat in the congregation. I talked to people. In one instance I went to a weekend event where members from around the Midwest had gathered in Chicago, and there were people there from many "Local Church" congregations. That was an all-day affair.

I stayed, and after the morning meeting I ate lunch with people. I talked to them, and more importantly I listened to their conversation and what they were talking about. Now, the meeting was out, and it was informal time, and I made some judgments about it. I found in talking about things like baseball scores yesterday and a movie one of them had seen, that these were just kind of normal things that my own church people would talk about over a church supper while they were drinking their last cup of coffee.

So those are the kinds of observations that I made.
JUDGE SEYRANIAN: *Did you take any of the local members and just simply say, "Look, I am doing a check, and I'd like to know your opinion. I don't want to take one of the elders. Do you feel you are held to this church by any forces? Do you think anything is being practiced upon you against your will?"*

DR. MELTON: I did that one night at a gathering where no elders were present, at a small group gathering. I have not done it particularly with one on one.

JUDGE SEYRANIAN: *How many were in that group?*

DR. MELTON: About ten people, and I asked them, and most of them had been converts from other groups.

JUDGE SEYRANIAN: *What was your evaluation to the answers that you got from these people?*

DR. MELTON: That they were fairly unsophisticated, and they did not know ahead of time that I was coming or who I was until toward the end of the meeting where something was said.

JUDGE SEYRANIAN: *Did they know anything about* The God-Men?

DR. MELTON: Oh, yes, they were quite aware of *The God-Men,* and they were quite aware of the case, but they seemed to be quite open.

JUDGE SEYRANIAN: *Did they feel very comfortable about that?*

DR. MELTON: Oh, very much so.

JUDGE SEYRANIAN: *So you would have an assessment that they weren't being held against their will, but they were there voluntarily?*

DR. MELTON: Oh, very much so. The group that met that night was quite varied. Two or three of them were businessmen and executives. One of them I know was running his own business. Another one was an owner of a print shop.

JUDGE SEYRANIAN: *Certainly nothing affecting their ability to earn a living and do well in that regard?*

DR. MELTON: The home we met in that night, I wish I lived that well.

MR. MORGAN: *Let me ask you a couple more questions along that line. In attending these meetings, can you describe generally the attitude of the people? Is it one that they appear to be happy, or do they appear to be under some form of bondage?*

DR. MELTON: Oh, they are definitely of that wing of Christianity that enjoys their faith. They do have a good time at worship. They have a much better time at worship, I must admit, than my Methodist Church on Sunday morning. I envy them in that.

MR. MORGAN: *Do they appear to be enjoying it as opposed to, as his Honor said, being there because they figure that will get them into the pearly gates?*

DR. MELTON: They are very much participating in the meetings. It is not a coerced participation. They are there because they want to be there and because they enjoy the worship experience. No, they are not being coerced. There is no sign that they are being coerced.

MR. MORGAN: *Have you had any opportunity to form any opinions as to the level of moral integrity of the people in that church?*

DR. MELTON: I have never had any reason to question it. Certainly there have never been any reports of members being involved in scandal or involved in criminal activity or anything that you would think of along this line.

I am currently investigating another group in Chicago right now which has a high percentage of members who are involved in some form of criminal activity. There is nothing like that that's ever even been hinted about the "Local Church."

EDITOR'S NOTE: *Dr. Melton was questioned concerning accusations of financial mismanagement only to establish the effect of such charges upon a reader. The charges were proven false by other witnesses involved in the financial transaction and also confirmed by the regional director of a Big Eight accounting firm, who reviewed the financial transaction in question and had full access to the records.*

MR. MORGAN: *Let me go on now to something else. Are you familiar with the allegation that talks about the $235,000 of Stuttgart?*

DR. MELTON: Yes.

MR. MORGAN: *Can you tell the court in your opinion what impact this charge and the statements that are made in there would have on Witness Lee?*

DR. MELTON: Well, the charge is basically that he is taking

money given to the church for a church project and using it for his own or for a small group in Anaheim's personal betterment, that there is a charge here of malfeasance, improper manipulation of funds.

MR. MORGAN: *What impact is that going to have on somebody like Witness Lee?*

DR. MELTON: Well, no church leader can survive for very long if the church members think he is using their money for purposes other than what they have been told they are giving it for.

MR. MORGAN: *You will notice also that immediately before that paragraph there is a mention of some other business transactions. Do you see that?*

DR. MELTON: Yes.

MR. MORGAN: *As an author can you give the court any opinion as to the effect that the paragraph about the $235,000 has in relation to these other events?*

DR. MELTON: Well, the implication–there is nothing said about Day Star of California [*a defunct California corporation*] that is particularly offensive in and of itself, but placed in the context of discussing financial matters, particularly Lee's personal financial matters, the accusation of malfeasance in this one case would tend to say, well, there is probably something going on in the financial matters discussed earlier. He's maybe siphoning off church funds to use in his personal business venture or something.

MR. MORGAN: *In your opinion, would that be a natural reaction for an average reader to think that, well, maybe there was something wrong with these other transactions as well?*

DR. MELTON: Certainly, given the continual accusations of so-called cult leaders; that is one of the things they do.

MR. MORGAN: *Another question now, Doctor. Have you found in your reading that* The God-Men *is being used as some sort of a source today even for other writers?*

DR. MELTON: I have been monitoring for at least a year now other anti-cult materials. As they have come out, they have continually quoted from or drawn from *The God-Men*. They are not fresh studies of the "Local Church." They are merely repetitions of material that's taken more or less blatantly from *The God-Men.*

MR. MORGAN: *In other words, whatever the lies are that are created here are being perpetuated by others just accepting that?*

DR. MELTON: Yes. I have a fairly thick file now of other materials that have been drawn directly from *The God-Men,* the Inter-Varsity edition.

MR. MORGAN: *Do you have an opinion as to why these other writers would just blindly accept what is in this book?*

DR. MELTON: This book is the only book-length study of Witness Lee by an outsider, that has had any kind of commercial publication. They have accepted it as authority, based in part because it is the only book available and also because it comes from SCP. SCP has built a good reputation overall in Christian circles.

MR. MORGAN: *Finally, could you kind of sum up in your opinion what the overall effect of this book has had and will have on Witness Lee and the "Local Church"?*

DR. MELTON: The effect of the book on Witness Lee is to have branded him as a false and deceptive teacher. The branding has gone on primarily among evangelical Christians where that is an important issue and to isolate him and his followers from the larger flow of the mainstream of the Christian church.

It has branded the "Local Church" as an heretical group which Christians should not get involved in and has led to, in particular, trouble on college campuses where they have tried to establish groups and evangelize.

MR. MORGAN: *That's all the questions I have.*

JUDGE SEYRANIAN: *I have just one question. To your knowledge, has anything been written and published that goes contrary to* The God-Men?

DR. MELTON: Not by anyone outside the church.

JUDGE SEYRANIAN: *Has there been anything published or written that's been by someone in the church?*

DR. MELTON: Oh, yes.

JUDGE SEYRANIAN: *Many or one or what?*

DR. MELTON: There are a handful of booklets. Mr. William

Freeman has published several book-length manuscripts, but they were very informally published and not very widely circulated. The two main items are two books that he wrote and Living Stream published answering charges of deviation of doctrine on the idea of mingling and the Trinity.

JUDGE SEYRANIAN: *Do those books challenge Mr. Duddy's statements and so forth?*

DR. MELTON: Both Mr. Duddy's statements and some of the earlier books were dealing directly with Jack Sparks' book which had become a matter of controversy a year or so before this one had. Jack Sparks' book was named *The Mindbenders*, and there was one pamphlet written in response called *Who Is the Real Mindbender?* The real problem is that these pamphlets are written and published within the confines of the "Local Church."

JUDGE SEYRANIAN: *In other words, they don't get a wide circulation.*

DR. MELTON: Christian bookstores would not carry them, not because of what they say, but because of who published them. Therefore, they could not get into bookstores to reach the people who *The God-Men* had reached.

JUDGE SEYRANIAN: *In other words, the Living Stream could not have the stature of SCP to get their books published like* The God-Men *was published?*

DR. MELTON: To a certain extent, SCP has the power to veto the circulation of material by their labeling of a group deviant or a cult.

JUDGE SEYRANIAN: *So the bookstores wouldn't carry their books?*

DR. MELTON: Bookstores won't carry it. The material of Watchman Nee that they carry is published by standard evangelical publishers. They will carry those items, but they would not carry anything that came from Living Stream.

JUDGE SEYRANIAN: *Do you feel that had it not been for* The God-Men *that Living Stream could have published a lot more books and gotten a wider circulation in their books?*

DR. MELTON: I don't know if they could have published a lot more titles. They could certainly have gotten a wider circulation. Christian bookstores would have found them, I think, acceptable books.

JUDGE SEYRANIAN: *Do you know whether or not* The God-Men *has had any effect on the growth of the "Local Church"?*

DR. MELTON: Only secondhand. I have heard reports that it has had effect. I know that it has blocked their growth on several campuses.

JUDGE SEYRANIAN: *In your Encyclopedia you don't do studies with respect to numbers as to how many members they have at this time, how many members at another time, or anything of that type where you would know something about whether or not the publication of this book has stymied the growth of this church?*

DR. MELTON: The Encyclopedia came out right at the same time that *The God-Men II* did, so in it there was not yet a chance to check to see if it had stymied growth or cut the trend of growth. There was a steady growth in the church up until the late seventies. I do not know from any research I have done as to exactly whether or not their growth overall has been stymied. I do know on several college campuses, where the book was distributed, their ability to evangelize was cut.

JUDGE SEYRANIAN: *In your opinion, knowing the structure of this church, do you feel that the members reading a book like The God-Men would cause them to turn away from their church or to have questions about their own church or to raise issues that they otherwise wouldn't have? In other words, do you feel that there was an effect within the "Local Church" itself by reason of the publication of* The God-Men?

DR. MELTON: No, I don't. I think the members of the "Local Church" were just offended by it.

JUDGE SEYRANIAN: *They were offended but didn't believe a word of it.*

DR. MELTON: "Why would somebody write a book that is so contrary to what we are doing and experiencing" would be their thinking. I think probably with those who were already members it may even have strengthened their faith. It is to the person on his way in who hasn't had a chance to experience what life is like inside the "Local Church," that is where it would raise questions, such as, "I don't want to get involved, with that much question."

JUDGE SEYRANIAN: *Yes, I understand. Thank you very much, Doctor.*

Chapter Three

THE TESTIMONY OF JOHN ALBERT SALIBA, Ph.D.

Mr. Morgan: *What is your calling?*

Dr. Saliba: I am a Catholic priest and a member of a religious order known as the Jesuits, and at the moment I hold the position of Associate Professor in the Department of Religious Studies at the University of Detroit.

Mr. Morgan: *How long have you held that position?*

Dr. Saliba: Since 1970 I have been teaching there. I have been Associate Professor since 1976 or thereabouts.

Mr. Morgan: *University of Detroit. Can you tell us something about it, what type of a school it is?*

Dr. Saliba: It is a school founded, to be precise, in 1877 by Jesuits, and now it is an inter-city school. It has about twenty percent minorities; only fifty percent are Catholic. There are 500 foreign students in a 6,000 body of students, and there is all variety of people on the campus. It is a nice place to be to have contact with different people and cultures and religious groups.

Judge Seyranian: *I went to your University of San Francisco, so I join in your feelings.*

Mr. Morgan: *That was the next question I was going to ask you. Is it somewhat like the University of San Francisco?*

Dr. Saliba: Yes, in fact, probably the University of San Francisco and University of Detroit, I think, are unique among the twenty-six Jesuit colleges there are throughout the country.3

Mr. Morgan: *Let me show you what's been marked as Exhibit 20, and I will ask if you can identify what that is.*

Dr. Saliba: That is my vitae plus a 1985 update.

MR. MORGAN: *I will offer that into evidence at this time, your Honor.*

JUDGE SEYRANIAN: *May be received.*

MR. MORGAN: *I just want to ask you a few things about it now, Father. First, can you tell us something about your educational background, where you got it?*

DR. SALIBA: I was born and educated first on the island of Malta, and I went to a Jesuit secondary school, and I joined the Jesuit order after high school. It was the normal time to join a religious order in the Catholic Church at that time.

I spent the first two years with the Jesuits in a program mainly of the spiritual training, and then about a year and a half or two years I did a bit more Latin, Greek, and some literature. Then after that I went to England and got a degree in a Jesuit seminary called Heythrop College.

MR. MORGAN: *Why to England? Why not Malta?*

DR. SALIBA: For two reasons. First, we were too small to run our own seminary, the Jesuits. Second, they wanted to give us the experience of being overseas. Malta is a small island. You may become very provincial if you live there all your life.

MR. MORGAN: *Okay, so you went to Heythrop.*

DR. SALIBA: Heythrop College. It has theological faculties of philosophy and theology. Our degrees are related to the Gregorian University in Rome, and Heythrop College has moved to London University and is actually a part of London University since 1970 or thereabouts.

MR. MORGAN: *Did you have any further formal education?*

DR. SALIBA: Yes. I did anthropology, what is known as social anthropology, at the University of Oxford, and there I spent another four years at Heythrop doing theology, and then I came to Catholic University in Washington and did my Ph.D. there in their Department of Religion.

MR. MORGAN: *What was your Ph.D. in?*

DR. SALIBA: In my Ph.D. I evaluated the work of a leading historian of religions by the name of Eliade, who was a household word in the United States in all departments of religion throughout the country, and I did an anthropological evaluation of his works.

MR. MORGAN: *Father, do you have some particular specialties today?*

DR. SALIBA: Yes, my specialty has been mainly anthropology of religion, and that is the study of comparative cultures, especially the more primitive ones, and over the last ten years my hobby has been studying new religious movements.

MR. MORGAN: *Did you ever become aware of SCP?*

DR. SALIBA: Yes, I had been in touch with their literature since probably '71, '72, or thereabouts.

MR. MORGAN: *Can you tell the court how it is you became aware of their literature?*

DR. SALIBA: Well, I spent the summer in Berkeley once, and I was around looking at different places, and if you were in Berkeley at the time, in the early seventies, you probably ran into what was known as the Christian World Liberation Front. You probably ran into them without planning to.

After that I just kept in touch. It was just like a hobby. I tell people, "Some people collect stamps. I go around and study these different religious groups."

MR. MORGAN: *Before we ever contacted you, did you make some study of some of the work of SCP?*

DR. SALIBA: Yes, in fact, my study of SCP is published in the *Journal of Ecumenical Studies,* which comes out of Temple University, and it is the only article in the respectable journal on the group.

MR. MORGAN: *Before I get to that, can you tell the court something about your publications? Have you had a number of publications in well-known publications?*

DR. SALIBA: I have. Besides my dissertation, which was published by Brill in Leiden, the Netherlands, I have published over the last twelve years a major article every year in extremely diverse journals, like, for instance, the *Theological Studies,* which is the leading Catholic theological journal, the *Journal of Ecumenical Studies,* the *Journal for the Scientific Study of Religion,* and now I also have a couple of articles coming out in a psychological journal.

JUDGE SEYRANIAN: *I notice you have quite a list of articles here.*

MR. MORGAN: *Father, what was the basic thrust of your article on SCP that was published?*

DR. SALIBA: Okay. Since I am basically a theologian and pastor, I was interested in how do you help people to cope with real problems they meet with when they join other groups. I was interested in the Christian response to these groups, so what I discovered first, by even looking at bookstores, was that the main responsible work was done by Evangelicals.

There was one semester when I wrote to lots of Bible colleges and seminaries to ask them what they were doing on the subject. And from the replies I got then, SCP came out frequently enough that I said they are a major influence. So then I zeroed in on them, because from a scholarly point of view it is much easier to work on a very definite body of literature rather than run all over the place. It is kind of like the ideal thing for a scholar to write an article on, when you have a body of literature there and you know you can read it all.

MR. MORGAN: *What conclusions did you draw about SCP's work from this study?*

DR. SALIBA: Well, SCP belongs to a small group of Evangelicals who have as their basic principle: Attack and destroy any group with which we don't agree. And that is their thrust of all the whole, everything you read.

I once thought of writing to them and suggesting they should find a different name for their group, maybe Spiritual Exterminators. It would be much more in line with what they were doing.

MR. MORGAN: *What about their work? You have indicated their policy, but what did you see from your study as far as their work?*

DR. SALIBA: Okay. Maybe I haven't read everything, but I have read a lot of what they have come out with, and nothing that I can see is publishable in a respectable journal.

In other words, I have evaluated articles for like, for

instance, the *Journal of Ecumenical Studies* and other journals. If any of their publications had been sent to me for evaluation, I would have told the editor, "Please, do not publish."

MR. MORGAN: *And why?*

DR. SALIBA: Well, because first of all, they don't have a methodology. You don't know how they go about their research. They have a principle that the only way you can find out what a group believes is to go to ex-members who are disgruntled and get information from them.

MR. MORGAN: *And what is wrong with that?*

DR. SALIBA: Well, you are going to get a very biased view. It is just like asking an ex-Catholic priest who was dissatisfied and left, "What about your life as a priest?" He is going to look back and say, "I found too many obstacles." While a person who is there in the group and happy, he is going to give you a much more plausible reason of what the group is all about.

MR. MORGAN: *Did you form any opinions as to whether they appear to have preconceived conclusions in their articles?*

DR. SALIBA: Yes, I have an inkling that SCP is always attacking Eastern groups. Anything which has even the slightest, remote idea of being Eastern, they are going to be on their guard, ready: this must be dangerous because it is Eastern. And in their approach, somehow it's gotten into their mind that the "Local Church" is Eastern, and oh my goodness, it is Eastern.

JUDGE SEYRANIAN: *Obviously in this trial we are learning that they attack the "Local Church." Can you tell me what other groups they were attacking?*

DR. SALIBA: TM, Transcendental Meditation. Unification Church. Yoga groups. Several of them. Zen. I can't remember any really good examples of the literature in which they say anything good about any group they put their hands on.

JUDGE SEYRANIAN: *In other words, most of their writings are attacking somebody?*

DR. SALIBA: It is negative, dangerous, and they have this vague idea it is Eastern mysticism, and this has a connotation. In fact, in my article I found out how they link all Eastern stuff with the devil. It is almost like a diabolical plot. They see the devil actually working to corrupt people by giving them Eastern religious groups, Yoga, and so on.

JUDGE SEYRANIAN: *Generally, do they use a large number of people to write these articles, or is it generally done by a very small group?*

DR. SALIBA: SCP has never had more than maybe ten at the most.

JUDGE SEYRANIAN: *That do all their writing?*

DR. SALIBA: Yes, and it is varied. A lot of movement of people, too. Some steady people across, but they have changed a bit too over the years.

JUDGE SEYRANIAN: *Have you ever done or found out what they use other than just talking to disgruntled members? Do they do something else?*

DR. SALIBA: They have never researched or rather had any reference to scholarly articles, and whenever once in a while you find a reference, it obviously had not influenced either their method or their conclusions.

Like, for instance, to give you an example, there is a recent book by Enroth on the guide to new religions, and there is a fairly decent chapter on what a cult is. He knows the sociological literature, but when you come to the last two pages of the chapter, he goes to calling a cult diabolical, which is hardly the result of a sociological investigation. So a scholarly work has not influenced them at all.

JUDGE SEYRANIAN: *I notice you have done a number of articles on cults and psychiatry. Would you feel that SCP has some kind of an attack on what they call cults?*

DR. SALIBA: Oh, yes.

JUDGE SEYRANIAN: *We have been trying to get definitions of a cult. How would you define it?*

DR. SALIBA: Before I say it, the word *cult* is one of those where there are hundreds of definitions. Even in sociology, you could probably have a library on just what has been written on what the word *cult* is. Probably the most commonly used definition or interpretation is: A cult is a marginal religious group. That definition has in itself no great derogatory meaning.

JUDGE SEYRANIAN: *What do you think the average layman on the street thinks of the word* cult?

DR. SALIBA: He is terrified of it.

JUDGE SEYRANIAN: *He doesn't have a small, marginal religious group theory, does he?*

DR. SALIBA: He thinks in terms of some mischievous group, evil, ready to control you, to take your money especially. In fact, I once said to a group of people, my belonging to a Jesuit order could also be used as being my belonging to a cult because, after all, I give my money to my order. I don't earn any money. It goes straight to my order. I could be accused just as well as belonging to a cult. I don't think I am.

JUDGE SEYRANIAN: *I don't think so either.*

MR. MORGAN: *Father, let me go on now. Did you at our request make certain studies regarding* The God-Men *publications as they relate to Witness Lee and also the "Local Church" itself?*

DR. SALIBA: The first time I heard of the "Local Church" was in fact through *The God-Men I*. I had taken that as an example in my essay of what I called a bad approach to new religious movements.

MR. MORGAN: *Why?*

DR. SALIBA: Because the methodology they used, in my opinion, and in the opinion, I think, of most scholarly work, is too negative, meaning instead of understanding, they are trying to debunk, and they debunk before they understand. So you say, "Now wait a minute. You can't figure out what they are saying if you start with the assumption that they are wrong." And I took that book as an example for the simple reason that it was the major book they had published. The rest were just kind of two-page leaflets.

JUDGE SEYRANIAN: The God-Men *was their first big publication?*

DR. SALIBA: Yes, as far as I know.

MR. MORGAN: *I believe, your Honor, the only two major*

publications they really had have been The God-Men I *and* The God-Men II.

DR. SALIBA: And lots of little leaflets, which in scholarly language were called junk. And then there are the SCP journals which I think are not named properly. They should be called the SCP Diatribes.

MR. MORGAN: *Let me ask you, tell us what you understood was your assignment from me and what you did in that regard.*

DR. SALIBA: Okay. I first had to go over *The God-Men II,* and go over some of the material they quoted, and then figure out whether they misrepresented the "Local Church" or not.

MR. MORGAN: *Did we also ask you to look into the "Local Church" itself?*

DR. SALIBA: Oh, you did, because I spent a lot of time visiting the church, especially in Detroit.

MR. MORGAN: *What was the reason for your examining the "Local Church" itself?*

DR. SALIBA: Well, I wanted to see—first of all, if you are studying any group, in anthropology they call it participant observation, and that means you go with the group as much as you can, of course, and you participate because you see that you share something in common, and I found that even though I am a Catholic, and I don't have the same theological views as the "Local Church," there were lots of things with which I would relate, so I could actually genuinely participate, at least at times, in their services.

I also wanted to see how people reacted, the dynamics of the group, like, for instance, when you read some of the stuff which is coming out on the cults, you hear about the manner of treatment of children, and I had that in my mind.

With this group there were lots of young families. They had baby-sitters look after the children while at service, and you could tell from the kids that they were very well treated, and I could see this just by going there, and what I did is I went for two months or so almost every Saturday, and the reason why I made this continuous, every weekend, is because it means you never saw the same members.

You could tell it wasn't like a group coming there almost

like a military academy, where every Saturday they all come. There was a variety. Some people were there all the time, but there were people who hadn't been there for some time, and they are coming back now, so I got a continuity of the church as the changes took place in it.

MR. MORGAN: *What was your opinion, then, as far as the church and the church people themselves?*

DR. SALIBA: I would say very average. I didn't notice anything which either worried me or which I put down under the label of strange. Now, of course, their services are a bit more lively than what I am accustomed to in a Sunday mass. I grant you that. But it is a matter of objective observation rather than anything else.

MR. MORGAN: *Okay.*

DR. SALIBA: I have to admit that some of the spirituality I found, that some of them were saying, they told me when I was a Jesuit novice twenty-five years ago, which was interesting.

MR. MORGAN: *Father, how about the book itself? What conclusion did you draw as far as* The God-Men *publication, as far as its truth and its fair representation of Witness Lee's teachings and the "Local Church"?*

JUDGE SEYRANIAN: *First of all, I believe you read Witness Lee's articles too?*

DR. SALIBA: Yes, I read about twelve books of Witness Lee plus lots of pamphlets, and I have read over 7,000 pages of deposition in the trial over the last two years.

MR. MORGAN: *Now what I want to know is, what your conclusions were about the book; does it fairly represent Witness Lee's teachings in the "Local Church" and the "Local Church" people?*

DR. SALIBA: Simple answer, no.

MR. MORGAN: *Can you tell us in what way it does not generally?*

DR. SALIBA: Well, the first thing is that the book takes Witness Lee out of his Christian context with no attempt to see him historically, which is a very great fault, because in our culture we try to use history to understand practically everything. Psychologically, sociologically, and even in the courts.

A history of the individual can give a very different

impression of what a person is like. But there is no attempt by the SCP to take the history of the "Local Church," where it came from, its roots and the Plymouth Brethren. It came all the way to contemporary Fundamentalism.

Then, of course, I got the impression that the conclusions were already set at the very start and that the author was skimming the pages. Oh, this fits into here, and then, oh yeah, this fits into here. So it was almost like what we call in academic circles a scissors-and-paste method of making a study: you cut those little quotations which you think will fit.

MR. MORGAN: *Did you find in your opinion that the book misrepresented the teachings of Witness Lee?*

DR. SALIBA: Yes, and what worries me more is that I couldn't see how a person could have done it who had some academic background as the author had. That is still a mystery to me.

MR. MORGAN: *Do you have any opinion as to whether the misrepresentations were done deliberately?*

DR. SALIBA: I hate to make judgments on people, but in this case I would be inclined to say they could not have been not deliberate.

JUDGE SEYRANIAN: *Father, was there anything in* The God-Men—*obviously I haven't read it—Is there anything in* The God-Men *that is complimentary to the "Local Church"?*

DR. SALIBA: I haven't found any. Okay, I think they praise them for their enthusiasm at one point.

JUDGE SEYRANIAN: *That's about it?*

DR. SALIBA: I made a list myself of what I call religious accusations and civil accusations, because theologically there are thousands of Christian churches, and we all disagree with one another. But I can disagree with you theologically without calling you names, and there is a lot of name calling.

JUDGE SEYRANIAN: *So in your opinion, then, the book does nothing in a constructive way as far as helping the "Local Church," but it is a book written strictly from the standpoint of trying to downgrade the "Local Church."*

DR. SALIBA: That is the impression, and I think any

person who read it would go as far away as he can from the "Local Church."

MR. MORGAN: *Father, what I want to ask you about now is the utilization by SCP and Mr. Duddy of Christ vs. Religion. Do you have that in mind?*

DR. SALIBA: Yes, I do.

MR. MORGAN: *First, as a Catholic priest, does that title give you some concern?*

DR. SALIBA: Not at all. If you have been doing some theology the last twenty years, you will realize that the idea of Christ versus religion was first developed in the Protestant circles and even some Catholic writings, and basically what they are trying to say is this, that over the centuries religion, Christianity included, has built up a lot of accretions, and obviously sometimes we have made the mistake of taking these accretions as being more important than the center theme of Christianity. And there is a constant battle going on in the Christian church over the last two thousand years fighting this thing, and as Dr. Melton mentioned, Karl Barth was probably the first one who crystallized it in this term: Christ versus Christianity, or religion.

MR. MORGAN: *Father, let me show you something from Duddy's writings, where he says:*

> The Local Church, therefore, not only fails to express social or moral consciousness, but explicitly counsels its members to avoid any such awareness.

Now, first, what do you understand that Mr. Duddy is saying to the reader?

DR. SALIBA: Well, first, my immediate reaction is that he tries to isolate them from society at large almost like: Whatever happens in society, forget it. Ivory towers.

Secondly, morality is obviously not inculcated. In other words, what you call the average thing, don't steal, et cetera, is not part of the awareness which the members are encouraged to develop.

MR. MORGAN: *Based upon your readings of Witness Lee, is this a true statement of his teachings?*

DR. SALIBA: No, it isn't.

MR. MORGAN: *What are the teachings of Witness Lee regarding morality and regarding social consciousness?*

DR. SALIBA: I think I am more sure on morality than on the other, but I will talk about both.

My impressions are from the reading of Lee's books and from hearing witnesses and people talking during the services that they accept basically the same morality I do, and it means the Ten Commandments plus also something beyond that. Meaning, you do not only try not to kill people but also try and be good to others too. Kind of like an added dimension to it.

From the view of social awareness I didn't have time to investigate, like, to what degree they involve themselves in politics, for instance.

MR. MORGAN: *Is that important?*

DR. SALIBA: Not particularly. You see there is a section of the Christian church, the more liberal, which looks on involvement in political and social matters as being almost as important as other matters. So if you want to evaluate it from that point of view, I suppose you could.

MR. MORGAN: *From the standpoint of your meeting the members of the church, what did you observe as far as their social consciousness?*

DR. SALIBA: Okay. In order to understand any other group or person, I usually try and find something similar in my life to which I can relate; and I thought, when I visited the "Local Church" for a couple of months' period, that there are some things I could compare to my own Jesuit community in Detroit, meaning, these were people who actually prayed together more than once every month or every year, so to speak, who ate together sometimes and discussed problems among themselves, very much as I would do in my community in Detroit.

There was no indication that they never talked to anybody else, but I would imagine that there was a community life among themselves which was more prominent than anything else.

MR. MORGAN: *Let me ask you this. Would it concern you or*

would you say that they had lost their social consciousness if they didn't particularly care to watch television?

DR. SALIBA: No. My reaction would be they wouldn't be missing much.

MR. MORGAN: *Let me go on to another one now. This is again one that I have covered with Dr. Melton, but I wanted the court to hear from you also. Duddy says:*

> Not only is the Local Church unwilling to exercise discipline, but, by intrinsic theological design, its ability to do so is foundationally inadequate because authority rests in conscious sensations from the Spirit–spirit whose voices may be many and varied.

First, Father, can you tell us what you understand Mr. Duddy is telling the readers there?

DR. SALIBA: It is not always easy to understand sometimes what Duddy is saying because he kind of like invents theological ways of putting stuff.

My conclusion is that apparently authority is not based on some kind of rule but rather comes from some kind of inner experience, kind of a "do what you will" mentality.

EDITOR'S NOTE: *Other witnesses testified, proving the falsity of the following alleged incident. Dr. Saliba's opinion here confirms that testimony.*

MR. MORGAN: *This follows the allegation of child rape, doesn't it?*

DR. SALIBA: Of course. If you have that kind of "authority," you could easily fall into that.

MR. MORGAN: *Mr. Duddy assigned blame to both Witness Lee's teaching and the "Local Church" for the child rape incident that is referred in here.*

DR. SALIBA: Yes.

MR. MORGAN: *First, do you have an opinion on Mr. Duddy's making that kind of a charge here?*

DR. SALIBA: My own opinion is, from my reading of the depositions, I don't think there is enough evidence for any person to make a charge like that. That is a serious charge, and if I had to do it or write something like that myself,

I would have rechecked and rechecked and rechecked the material, because it's really not something you write down.

MR. MORGAN: *And he didn't do that, did he?*

DR. SALIBA: From his own deposition, apparently he didn't. It was almost like: I say something, and you accept it, and then I tell you I accept it because you have said it. That is the process which is going on all the time: everybody confirming everybody else, and it is very hard to figure out where the actual rumor started. You can't pinpoint it.

MR. MORGAN: *What about Witness Lee's teaching? From your reading, is Witness Lee's teaching such that they are unable to exercise discipline and to even know that they need it?*

DR. SALIBA: In my worst dream it wouldn't occur to me that is the case.

MR. MORGAN: *Tell us what your understanding is of Witness Lee's teachings regarding morality.*

DR. SALIBA: Witness Lee is basically very biblically oriented; he insists on the Bible which is the primary authority, which is very Protestant in spirit. There is nothing new with that. He accepts the basic morality of the Old Testament and New Testament, and I find practically no difference between my views on morality and his.

MR. MORGAN: *In your opinion, what is the effect of these kinds of charges against a Bible teacher such as Witness Lee?*

DR. SALIBA: They ruin his reputation. In a small church like the "Local Church," there are different social and psychological dynamics which operate than, say, in a large denomination. And in the case like this, first of all, it ruins his reputation. When I talked to Witness Lee myself, I think he was practically brokenhearted over the matter, and if I were a member of the church—and I probably would not have believed it—but if I had doubts, I would have started thinking of leaving.

MR. MORGAN: *What about the rest of the Christian community? What effect would these kinds of charges have on Witness Lee's reputation?*

DR. SALIBA: I would label him with the nice label C-U-L-T, *cult*, which includes beware, stay away from, and don't ever relate to those people because there is something wrong with that group.

MR. MORGAN: *Does that apply to the church as well as Witness Lee?*

DR. SALIBA: The church itself, because when you join a group, you are actually not joining a person or a leader. You are joining a group as such.

Most members of the "Local Church" don't sit with Mr. Lee very often.

MR. MORGAN: *How about looking at these two different quotes used in* The God-Men. *It says:*

> *In my Christian dictionary there is not such a word as "evil," nor is there such a word as "good"! From the beginning to the end my Christian dictionary contains only one word—"Christ"! I understand neither good nor evil. I do not want help to do good; I only want Christ!*
>
> *…Spontaneously we will bear fruit. This is the missing key. Trying to do good is a real temptation and a great distraction from experiencing Christ.* [The Economy of God, p. 38]

> *Eventually, there is no right or wrong, no yes or no—only Jesus!…There is no law, no teaching, no regulations—only Jesus. And not a Jesus in doctrine but a Jesus who is so living, so instant, and so present.* [Christ vs. Religion, pp. 63-64]

Now, first, those are quotes taken from Witness Lee's statements, is that right?

DR. SALIBA: Yes, they are.

MR. MORGAN: *Can you tell the court what you understand Mr. Duddy is attempting to convey to the readers here?*

DR. SALIBA: Something which is very common in Christian spirituality, meaning, the key element in Christian life is a personal relationship with Christ.

MR. MORGAN: *What I want to know is what Mr. Duddy is trying to convey to the reader?*

DR. SALIBA: He is trying to say that if you join the "Local Church," all you need to do is develop this kind of experience, and then do whatever you want. Don't worry about what is right or wrong.

MR. MORGAN: *But didn't Witness Lee say, "In my Christian dictionary there is not such a word as 'evil'"?*

DR. SALIBA: I know, because the reason is this: If you really accept Christ, then you never really worry about the problem of doing evil. You automatically do good.

JUDGE SEYRANIAN: *That reminds me of when I was in Sunday school, we had a minister—I was a Presbyterian before I became a Catholic—and the teaching was, if you loved Christ, you could do anything you want, and we thought that meant we could go out and do anything, until he explained that the things you want to do, you wouldn't do if you loved Christ.*

DR. SALIBA: That is what Witness Lee is saying, and, your Honor, Saint Augustine is responsible for that saying. He is quoted as saying, Love and do whatever you want.

JUDGE SEYRANIAN: *I suppose that's true.*

MR. MORGAN: *Did you find in your readings that Mr. Duddy took these statements out of context?*

DR. SALIBA: Not only out of context. I get the impression they were twisted around to mean what he wanted them to mean.

MR. MORGAN: *And then are you saying that this isn't something that was done inadvertently; this was done deliberately?*

DR. SALIBA: Again, I don't like judging people, but I cannot honestly see how this could have been a genuine, innocent mistake.

MR. MORGAN: *Let me go to another quote from* The God-Men. *I will ask you to read to yourself, and then I will ask you some questions about it.*

> *Often in reading Lee, you would think church government to be unimportant, since he derides forms and organizations so consistently, offering in their stead "spontaneous," organic growth. In practice, however, he does establish an authoritative eldership and diaconate of sorts, composed of those who are "spiritually advanced." They wield strong authority over ordinary church members.*
>
> *"Toward one who has the ministry of the Holy Spirit we should really be careful! You may freely criticize those who walk on the street, but you should not freely criticize nor purposely dispute with one who has the ministry of the Holy*

Spirit...as soon as you criticize him and dispute with him, his ministry toward you is finished." [The Knowledge of Life, p. 215]

> Such authoritative leadership exerts great leverage in the church member's life, generating intense dependency on the leader's approval in both personal matters (home life, vocation, and the like) and church affairs. To differ with a leader's counsel puts one in a "soulish" predicament, adrift from the spiritual flow of church life, so one understandably prefers submission with its security and approval to the exercise of personal judgment and individual decision.

Again, can you tell the court what you understand Mr. Duddy is attempting to convey to the reader?
DR. SALIBA: Okay, this talks about authority in the church, and the idea here is that this is a very authoritarian group, where Witness Lee rules more or less like a despot, and where the elders are more or less little despots in their own little fields, and they control everything, and you are just merely submissive to them.
MR. MORGAN: *Doesn't he quote Witness Lee there in the middle paragraph, that you should not freely criticize and so on?*
DR. SALIBA: Yes, he does.
MR. MORGAN: *Again, does that fairly represent Witness Lee's teachings?*
DR. SALIBA: No, I don't think so. Again, we are not encouraged to criticize the pope, and it is not an imposition for us. We don't feel it that way. I wouldn't conclude that the pope is my dictator. So I think he is talking here of the way people should relate within the same community, and within a community the best relationship is not one of confrontation and criticism but actually dialogue and exchanging views and pointing out matters without a public debate, which I think is the correct way to do it.
MR. MORGAN: *And did you understand that is the way Witness Lee teaches it?*
DR. SALIBA: That is my impression.
MR. MORGAN: *Here Mr. Duddy has put it in there to make it appear that Witness Lee is saying you don't argue with the elders.*

DR. SALIBA: Yes. I remember an incident at one of the meetings I attended, and one of the elders at the end of the service was encouraging people to go to a regional meeting. He was encouraging them without an imposition that I can tell you.

MR. MORGAN: *In your visits to the "Local Church" have you observed any conduct that would appear to be that of autocratic rule or despots or anything of that sort?*

DR. SALIBA: No, and I have been trained to observe all that stuff, because they teach in anthropology to use your eyes and ears like antennae. You are watching everything you see, so I was watching the mood of the people. I was watching how they were relating to each other. I was noticing everything. I was like a hawk sometimes.

JUDGE SEYRANIAN: *By the way, in one of these paragraphs, Father, it says they are ascribing to Witness Lee that he controls the home life and the vocations of his followers. Did you experience anything like that?*

DR. SALIBA: I saw no evidence of it.

JUDGE SEYRANIAN: *Or in his writings?*

DR. SALIBA: There is nothing. But again if you think in terms of the "Local Church" as a community, very much as a resort is a community, I think you will understand what is happening much more easily.

If you look upon it as a huge church where people are going there once a month, then you will not really get a good glimpse of the actual spirituality and dynamics of the group.

People are always afraid when they see great commitment, because great commitment means you put limitations on yourself. But once you are committed, then limitations are never that damaging to you.

If I may give you an example from my own vocation, there are many Catholics and non-Catholics who are surprised how not being married isn't a great sacrifice for me, and my reaction is, it is a sacrifice, but I don't really feel it because I am committed, so that is the reason why I'd rather talk to people in the group rather than outside the group, because outside the group they have lost their commitment, they have lost their vocation. So when they look back to their past, they tend to look at those years or months as a waste of time.

JUDGE SEYRANIAN: *I agree with you.*

DR. SALIBA: My complaint with the SCP literature has always been that they don't understand commitment, they have no idea of religious experience, what it means, and therefore, they misunderstand much of the groups they study.

MR. MORGAN: *Did you learn in your reading that Witness Lee's method of counseling or advising is to tell them to pray and find the answer?*

DR. SALIBA: Yes. Several times, actually.

JUDGE SEYRANIAN: *Mr. Morgan, are all of the people that references are made to in* The God-Men *people that have left the church?*

MR. MORGAN: *Yes.*

JUDGE SEYRANIAN: *None of them were participating members of the church at the time the book was written?*

MR. MORGAN: *It is basically three or four, and what we are going to do at some point is put in evidence that Mr. Duddy attempted to get from them affidavits to substantiate what they were saying, and they refused to give them to him.*

JUDGE SEYRANIAN: *I think you had made that comment before.*

DR. SALIBA: Your Honor, also in SCP newsletters, when they are investigating a group, they very often put a note asking for ex-members to contact them. It is a very common practice.

MR. MORGAN: *We do know from our discovery that Mr. Squires, and he may be here today, he's in the back there, sent out questionnaires. They have a mailing list of ex-members of the "Local Church," and they sent out questionnaires, and it is important to us in certain phases because they didn't get any negative responses back on certain things they were looking for.*

JUDGE SEYRANIAN: *Father, with respect to cults and the charge of a group as being a cult, do you feel that it is impossible over a period of time to ever eradicate that classification that is placed on you, right or wrong or otherwise?*

DR. SALIBA: It is very difficult, given the climate in our society. In fact, the social stigma—I can't see it in my lifetime.

JUDGE SEYRANIAN: *I agree with you. No matter what people's connotation?*

DR. SALIBA: Unfortunately, we tend to believe something of a strange rumor much more readily than something good.

MR. MORGAN: *I just have a few more, Father. This paragraph from* The God-Men *says:*

> The Local Church uses certain psycho-spiritual techniques to guide the experience of its members into a sense of mystical transcendence and collective solidarity. These techniques are based upon principles of mental manipulation that are as old as humanity, and as contemporary as est or Transcendental Meditation.

Then it goes on to basically calling on the name of the Lord and pray-reading.

First, what do you understand Mr. Duddy is trying to convey to the readers there? Actually, this is Mr. Alexander, but what do you understand?

DR. SALIBA: What he is saying is the common accusation against many religious groups, that they manipulate you, brainwash you, and then more or less you become, to use an extreme term but used in literature, a living zombie, so to speak.

MR. MORGAN: *Any evidence that in the teachings or in the church there is any mental manipulation, brainwashing?*

DR. SALIBA: None at all.

MR. MORGAN: *These practices, the pray-reading and calling on the name of the Lord, you have seen those, have you not?*

DR. SALIBA: Yes.

MR. MORGAN: *Have you participated in them?*

DR. SALIBA: Not in pray-reading. It was a little bit unusual. I am not used to the average "Local Church" meeting with everybody participating, and there is no prescribed order of prayer as there would be in my tradition. I don't feel as comfortable as in my own tradition, which is understandable, but it doesn't bother me. I wasn't surprised or upset or anything.

MR. MORGAN: *Did you see anything about that that created mental manipulation or brainwashing?*

DR. SALIBA: I can't figure out anything which would.

MR. MORGAN: *In the book they talk about the fact that this repetition, saying the verses over and over again, will somehow get the person hyperventilating and then get them into an altered state of consciousness, and then Witness Lee can swoop down and manipulate their minds.*

DR. SALIBA: The only thing I notice if somebody is hyperventilating and you are there after he is hyperventilated, you will see it. That is a physical phenomenon. I never saw anybody hyperventilating in any sense of the word. And after the meeting they talked like ordinary human beings. So they were not waiting for Witness Lee to more or less say something for them to do.

MR. MORGAN: *What about the repetition? Do you see anything wrong in that?*

DR. SALIBA: No. Repetitious prayer is often common in Christianity too. The old tradition of saying the Jesus Prayer is probably fifteen hundred years old. In the Catholic Church we say the rosary, which is repetitious.

And the important thing is, this is what I think the book doesn't either understand or ignores or whatever, they try to compare pray-reading with the mantra. But that is not quite the case, because the mantra is magical, meaning you don't even have to know what it means for it to work, and if you go to TM, for instance, they tell you that you don't even have to believe in what they say or understand the mantra. It will work.

What the "Local Church" members were pray-reading were the sections of the Gospel from the New Testament in English, not in a language nobody understood. So they knew what they were doing. So I don't see the similarity except that it is repetitious prayer.

MR. MORGAN: *Father, what in your opinion does the cover of* The God-Men *portray?*

DR. SALIBA: I get an idea of something of a person very powerful and hypnotic looking at me through eyes, which you don't see the eyes, so there is an element of, "You are not sure who I am."

There is kind of a seductive smile on his face. And then you have those pictures on the glasses. One is a temple. It is that which comes to me. I don't know what they had in mind, and the other is people jumping around.

It wouldn't attract me to the person. There is no doubt about it.

MR. MORGAN: *In your opinion what has been the total impact of these publications on Witness Lee and the "Local Church"?*

DR. SALIBA: Okay. I am not sure how much it has affected their members. I didn't make any study of that. I can't inform you on that matter. I would say in general it is negative because it could also instill some doubts in some people probably.

It also has caused them a lot of, I would say, internal trouble, because here you are being publicly, in writings and on TV, accused. I would never have heard probably of the "Local Church" if it had not been for the book, so that is the only book which there is on the "Local Church." It is really a very negative effect.

MR. MORGAN: *When you add to it the fact that Witness Lee is a Bible teacher, has been a Bible teacher for fifty years, what does that do to him and his reputation?*

DR. SALIBA: I would say it destroys it.

MR. MORGAN: *In the course of your reading, did you come across some teaching by Witness Lee on the book of Revelation?*

DR. SALIBA: Yes, I have.

MR. MORGAN: *Simply, if possible, what is the book of Revelation?*

DR. SALIBA: In the Catholic Church we often call it the Apocalypse, which, in fact, is the Greek word meaning revelation. It is a very symbolic book which talks on the seven churches. It is the most difficult book in the Bible, in my opinion. There are umpteen books and commentaries on the book of Revelation.

MR. MORGAN: *In the course of your reviewing that, you saw Witness Lee when he was explaining the interpretation of that book, did you not?*

DR. SALIBA: Yes.

MR. MORGAN: *In the course of that, did he say things that were uncomplimentary to the Catholic religion?*

DR. SALIBA: Yes, there is a common explanation, I forgot the exact chapter in Revelation where it refers to Babylon, and Babylon is interpreted to be Rome, and then the next step is Rome being the Catholic Church.

MR. MORGAN: *Is that something that is unique with Witness Lee?*

DR. SALIBA: No, it is fairly common among Fundamentalists. It wasn't the first time I came across it.

MR. MORGAN: *So when you saw that, did that in any way affect your ability to evaluate everything here.*

DR. SALIBA: No, because, first of all, Witness Lee doesn't harp against the Catholic Church all the time. It is not like some evangelists do on television. So it occurs occasionally, and I remember one quote, but I don't remember the exact location where he says, Love everybody, Protestant and Catholic included; so I said, At least Witness Lee may interpret Revelation against my church, but he doesn't hate me.

MR. MORGAN: *Finally, in your review of Mr. Duddy's writings and Witness Lee's books, did you find that Mr. Duddy consistently took Witness Lee's quotes out of context?*

DR. SALIBA: Oh yes, I would have to look for exceptions.

MR. MORGAN: *Did you find that he also distorted the use of Witness Lee's quotes?*

DR. SALIBA: Yes, I think he did very often.

MR. MORGAN: *Thank you. I have nothing further.*

JUDGE SEYRANIAN: *Thank you very much, Father.*

Chapter Four

THE TESTIMONY OF
EUGENE VAN NESS GOETCHIUS, Ph.D., Th.D.

MR. MORGAN: *What is your calling?*
DR. GOETCHIUS: I am an Episcopal priest. I am Professor of Literature and Interpretation of the New Testament and Professor of Biblical Languages at the Episcopal Divinity School, and I also have a lectureship at Harvard University, also in Interpretation of the New Testament.
MR. MORGAN: *Is the Episcopal Divinity School affiliated with any university or college?*
DR. GOETCHIUS: Yes, sir, it is affiliated with Harvard and has been for many years. It is affiliated with the Weston School of Theology, which is a Jesuit Theologate. It is affiliated with the Boston Theological Institute, which is a consortium of, I think, eleven various denominations including Greek Orthodox, two or three Roman Catholic, one quite conservative Protestant, and that's about it, I guess.
(Curriculum Vitae of Eugene Van Ness Goetchius marked for identification as Plaintiff's Exhibit 21.)
MR. MORGAN: *Let me show you what's been marked as Exhibit 21, and I will ask you if you can identify what that is.*
DR. GOETCHIUS: That is my curriculum vitae.
    MR. MORGAN: *I will offer that into evidence, if I may.*
    JUDGE SEYRANIAN: *It may be admitted.*
MR. MORGAN: *Just a few questions now about it. First, can you tell us something about your educational background?*
DR. GOETCHIUS: Well I never got out of it, I suppose, for one thing. I have been in school all my life. I think I was probably afraid not to stay there.

But I went to the University of Virginia, as you see, for ten years where I received four degrees. What happened between 1941, when I got my B.A., and 1947, when I got my master of science, you may recall the unpleasantness of World War II, during which time I was teaching navigation in the Navy and meteorology to the Army Air Force, and so by doing that I got a degree in mathematics. So then I had to go back to Germany, and when I finished there, I felt called to the ministry. After finishing the Ph.D. in Germanic languages, I went to the seminary, and after having taught a couple of years in between, I went on to get another degree, another doctorate in New Testament interpretation.

MR. MORGAN: *What do you teach now?*

DR. GOETCHIUS: Well, I teach an introductory course in New Testament interpretation. I have been doing that since around 1963. I teach it in conjunction with a Jesuit professor and a Harvard professor who's also sometimes a Jesuit. This sometimes makes my position very interesting, but the Anglican position has always been an interesting one, in between everybody else.

I also teach introductory Greek and secondary Greek at seminary and fourth-year Greek at Harvard, and I give a course on the Holy Spirit.

MR. MORGAN: *You have listed all your articles that you have written in the Exhibit, is that correct?*

DR. GOETCHIUS: I believe so. I am not very prolific, I am afraid, partly because of the field I am most interested in, which is grammar. I have written a Greek grammar, I am preparing to write a second-year grammar, and I have done work on a dictionary, which is still in alpha.

MR. MORGAN: *Doctor, let me do this. Let me ask you now about when you first became aware of the "Local Church."*

DR. GOETCHIUS: Yes, it was through my teaching of Greek that this happened. One of the members of the church in Newton, Massachusetts telephoned me and said he would like to take Greek, and I assured him that he could register at the Episcopal Seminary. He said that would be inconvenient because I taught it at nine o'clock in the morning four days a week, and besides he had a number of friends who also wanted to do it. After some backing and filling I agreed to teach them on Friday evenings from 7:30 to 9:30.

MR. MORGAN: *Can you give us an idea as to when that was?*

DR. GOETCHIUS: That was in the fall of 1983.

MR. MORGAN: *At that time had you had any awareness of either Witness Lee or the "Local Church"?*

DR. GOETCHIUS: None.

MR. MORGAN: *How long did this class last then?*

DR. GOETCHIUS: Well, we finished the introductory grammar course in one semester, then we did reading in the New Testament for the following two semesters, and this is at the present the fourth semester. I am on sabbatical. They wanted to continue, but I was unable to do that.

MR. MORGAN: *About how many from the "Local Church" attended this class?*

DR. GOETCHIUS: We began with, I think, eighteen, and we ended with about a dozen.

MR. MORGAN: *In addition to teaching them, did you have an occasion to be with them socially?*

DR. GOETCHIUS: Yes. During the first semester they invited me, socially in the strict sense then, and during the first semester they invited me and my wife to their meeting hall in Newton for dinner. In the second semester we invited them with their children to come to our house on Cape Cod and spend the day, which they did.

MR. MORGAN: *Prior to my associates' contacting you to assist us in this litigation, had you formed any opinions about these members of the "Local Church"?*

DR. GOETCHIUS: They were all bright; all the students that I had were computer people. They were all engaged in that. They were the most highly motivated students that I think I had. In one semester they finished my book of New Testament Greek in two hours a week, which my regular class finished in four hours a week. I think they did better.

MR. MORGAN: *Were you able to form any opinion as to their theological beliefs?*

DR. GOETCHIUS: Well, I didn't; since I never heard of the "Local Church," I did ask them at first what church they belonged to, and they told me the church in Newton, to which my natural response was, which church in Newton. The answer to that I didn't understand, and so later they brought me one of Witness Lee's books, which was translated into Greek, which I thought was rather nice. I then realized, from seeing that, this was a connection with Watchman Nee, whom I had heard of before through one of my own Episcopal students who gave me his book called *The Normal Christian Life.*

MR. MORGAN: *Then were you requested by me to make certain studies?*

DR. GOETCHIUS: Yes.

MR. MORGAN: *Would you tell the court what you did in that regard?*

DR. GOETCHIUS: Well, I read the Duddy manuscript, and I tried to check as many of the references that he made as I possibly could. I read at least a dozen books by Witness Lee. I have kept notes on the same. I saw six tapes of Witness Lee.

I neglected to say, because you asked me socially, how I met them. I went out to a meeting of the church in Newton and heard Witness Lee in person. I met him, and we had a very brief correspondence, because I thought that his presentation that night, which lasted a couple of hours, was a very concise presentation of the Christian faith, or as represented by the Bible.

He traced right straight through. The only thing I missed was the book of Revelation. I should have stayed for that, but that was actually postponed until the next day.

MR. MORGAN: *After doing that, first, did you form any opinions as to the theology of Witness Lee and the "Local Church"?*

DR. GOETCHIUS: Yes. This was before I had heard of the book, when I heard him. My impression was that here was a church which was more enthusiastic than "God's frozen people," which Episcopalians are referred to as, but certainly within the limits of orthodoxy, possibly further in than some Episcopalians.

MR. MORGAN: *When you reviewed the manuscript and Witness Lee's writings, what did you find as far as the manuscript representing the teachings and practices of the "Local Church"?*

DR. GOETCHIUS: Well, my initial impression from a very rapid reading of the book and before I actually read the teachings of Witness Lee, but from knowing the members of the church, my initial impression of the book was that this was a very sloppy piece of scholarship. Then after I read the books of Witness Lee and compared passages, I became convinced, sadly, that this was a deliberate, careful misrepresentation of the teachings of Witness Lee.

MR. MORGAN: *I know the court has heard a lot now, but can you give us just some examples of what you thought were deliberate?*

DR. GOETCHIUS: Well, one has been touched on several times, that is, Witness Lee's approach to the Bible as being unimportant. A very casual reading of Witness Lee's works will show that every passage that he writes is developed from an exegesis of text, book after book. He has a study of Genesis. I haven't actually seen straight through the Bible, but Genesis, Exodus, Romans, First Corinthians, and Ephesians.

All of his teaching is based directly on the Bible. Many times he says, as you had up there quoted, "I will die for the Bible." That opinion could be reflected many times in his works.

Again, the thing that really set me on my ear was the idea that the members of the "Local Church" were immoral. I had these people in my house. I taught them for a semester, and in the second semester I met them in my house, and I had been to their house, and they had been at my house on the Cape. They met my family.

If I had formed an opinion of them as far as morality was concerned, the modern technical term that comes to mind is square. Certainly the people that I had known, being very accustomed to the Harvard Square area, I would have rated them very high, I suppose. But these were people who were well above average in intelligence, and it seemed to me that they were the kind of people that I felt very much at home with.

MR. MORGAN: *Did you see any evidence of mental manipulation by Witness Lee or others upon the people that you were training?*

DR. GOETCHIUS: Never.

MR. MORGAN: *The term* sensuous theology *that we brought up, is that an accepted theological term?*

DR. GOETCHIUS: I have never seen it before except in this book. Witness Lee does not use it himself. I thought that perhaps the term was derived from his work, and so I looked for it, and I didn't find it, and I made inquiry and was assured it doesn't occur. It is a strange term to use, I think.

MR. MORGAN: *What do you understand that Mr. Duddy and SCP are trying to convey by that term?*

DR. GOETCHIUS: Well, I had to go look up the word because what I understood that he was trying to do was to play on the meaning of the words *sensuous* and *sensual*. *Sensuous* in its broad sense means pertaining to the senses. I think that might be allowed. One of the synonyms listed in my dictionary is *sensual,* which is sexual pleasure.

I had a feeling that Duddy was using the term deliberately. That was the feeling I got from reading the book, especially when it was associated with charges of immorality. It is true that Witness Lee does teach an experiential approach, and that is the word I think would have been used in this case.

MR. MORGAN: *How about the concept of "moral pygmies"?*

DR. GOETCHIUS: I have not read B. B. Warfield on the subject, so I interpreted it the logical way. If I called someone a mental pygmy, I would see them to be a person of short intelligence. A moral pygmy would be somebody who was short on morals. Better than an immoral pygmy. I take this to be insulting in describing a person who is lacking in moral perception and understanding.

MR. MORGAN: *Did you see anything in Witness Lee's teachings that could justify somebody making a charge of lack of moral understanding?*

DR. GOETCHIUS: On the contrary. In Witness Lee's discussion on morality, he says in a number of places that the righteousness of his followers should exceed the righteousness of the Pharisees.

Witness Lee says that members of the church should not merely fulfill the law but should have a higher morality. That is really what he is teaching when it says the law doesn't matter. He doesn't mean you don't have to live up to the law. He means that you must go beyond that, and he makes that point a number of times.

MR. MORGAN: *What in your opinion is the effect of these publications on Witness Lee and the "Local Church" in the Christian community?*

DR. GOETCHIUS: Well, if I believe it, I would never have anything to do with Witness Lee, certainly. I would avoid him. If I had read the book before these people came to take Greek, I wouldn't have accepted them. I would have made some excuse and done something else, because I would have just as soon not have them around.

MR. MORGAN: *Why is that?*

DR. GOETCHIUS: Because of the association with C-U-L-T which is the dirty four-letter word of the afternoon. Because I have had very unfortunate experiences with cults. My godson, whose father is a professor of theology at the seminary I teach in, was wafted away by the Children of God, and he still is a member of that. Since I have four sons, I would not want to be in a position of having members of a cult in my house.

MR. MORGAN: *Based upon your experience and knowledge, is that pretty much the feeling throughout the country, that parents are genuinely afraid of their children getting into cults?*

DR. GOETCHIUS: Well, I can only speak for the parents that I know, and in the past few years people with teenage children have been upset about this. Yes.

MR. MORGAN: *Would you agree that if a parent read the SCP publication* The God-Men *that this would strike somewhere in their heart?*

DR. GOETCHIUS: It certainly would.

MR. MORGAN: *What about the term* God-men? *What is the significance of that in your mind?*

DR. GOETCHIUS: Well, in my mind I think I understand what Witness Lee means by that, because he does use the term.

Christ means for us to be more than good men. He means for us to be God-men. I believe that is a reasonable paraphrase of something that Witness Lee said.

But he is referring to a terminology and to a teaching that goes very far back in Christianity, in fact, to the New Testament itself. In the Gospel of John where Jesus tells his disciples, "I am in the Father and the Father in Me...and We shall come and dwell in you," and the phrase *God-man* occurs in, I guess it is, Anselm, but I mean referring to human beings. Athanasius, who is certainly the father of orthodoxy, teaches that God became man so that we might become divine. It is certainly not a heretical remark, but I think Duddy is meaning that as quite something else.

MR. MORGAN: *What do you understand that Duddy and SCP are attempting to convey to the readers by using the term* The God-men?

DR. GOETCHIUS: They are trying to make me think that here are people who think a great deal more highly of themselves than they ought to think, who think they are beyond the call of human morality. That is in the pattern of the book.

God, presumably, can do no wrong. So, if you are a God-man, presumably, you can do no wrong either.

EDITOR'S NOTE: *Dr. Goetchius was questioned concerning accusations of financial mismanagement to establish the effect of such charges upon a reader. The falsity of these charges was established by other witnesses.*

MR. MORGAN: *What about the charge of financial impropriety? What in your opinion could that have by way of an effect on a Bible teacher such as Witness Lee?*

DR. GOETCHIUS: It would certainly be devastating if it could be substantiated. There must be objective proof one way or the other, but the charge even if not substantiated would be devastating.

MR. MORGAN: *How about the cover? What does the cover conjure up in your mind, the cover of* The God-Men II?

DR. GOETCHIUS: Well, it is certainly a caricature. I know Witness Lee, so I would recognize him, but if I hadn't known him, I would recognize it with difficulty, even having seen him. It is a person who is sneering; it is someone I would not want to meet, not somebody whose house I would go to and have tea with, which I did with Witness Lee.

JUDGE SEYRANIAN: *Father, when you read this book,* The God-Men, *did you get the feeling that there was a charge that the "Local Church" was in a form of a cult? Before you heard about this trial or anything else.*

DR. GOETCHIUS: When I read the book?

JUDGE SEYRANIAN: *Yes.*

DR. GOETCHIUS: Yes. I don't think that the book actually calls—uses the term *cult* about the church; but I also read the German version of it, and in that, at the end of that, there is a reference by simple juxtaposition to the Jim Jones business in South America, which is certainly calculated to give someone like myself who remembers the picture on *Time* magazine of all these people lying around dead, here is another thing of that kind.

JUDGE SEYRANIAN: *Suppose you put the German book aside and make reference to* The God-Men *in English. Do you feel that book, just reading the book itself, would give you the feeling that the "Local Church" is a cult?*

DR. GOETCHIUS: Yes, I would, because of the discussions of manipulation. That would be it. To my mind it seems to me—as has been indicated, a cult is something very hard to describe, and I would have to begin more or less the way Dr. Melton did by saying the principal cults are thus and such. The one I have known of most closely is the Children of God who certainly bent this child's mind, and those that I have heard of, the Hare Krishna people that I meet in Harvard Square, and the one that occurs to me most above all is the Unification Church, which worries me because they have so many front organizations. You never know when you are dealing with them. That, I suppose, is the one I would think of when I saw that picture, because it is clearly an oriental face, and I would think Reverend Moon. That would bother me.

JUDGE SEYRANIAN: *Do you feel that in this day and age if someone gets the feeling that something is a cult that they'd have a very negative feeling by the use of that word?*

DR. GOETCHIUS: I do think so.

JUDGE SEYRANIAN: *What would you think the average lay person, not people with any theology background or understanding as the witnesses I have heard, but just the average person, if he hears that some church is branded a cult, what would he think?*

DR. GOETCHIUS: It seems his reaction would be quite negative. *Cult* is certainly a derogatory term.

JUDGE SEYRANIAN: *Especially in this day and age.*

DR. GOETCHIUS: Yes, very much so. *Cult* in antiquity could be used in a perfectly flat, unemotional way when you talk about the cult of the Romans and the Greeks, but that is not what it means now.

MR. MORGAN: *Let me ask you a few things about your observations of the members of the "Local Church." First, what did you observe as far as their being a family and family-oriented?*

DR. GOETCHIUS: They are extremely family-oriented. They have the best behaved children that I have ever met, en masse, certainly.

When they came to my house at the Cape, there were twelve families. Twelve men and their wives and an uncountable number of children.

The "Local Church" may be a small church now, but just wait. It was raining that day, and we had to stay in the house, and it was all right. There wasn't a lot of crying, neither was any child under any adult's thumb. There was a lot of smiling. We sat around and read books to them. We sang hymns out of the "Local Church" hymnal, which they had thoughtfully brought along with them, and they gave me a copy, and I must say if you think the theology of the "Local Church" is unorthodox you should read the hymns.

Their hymns are much more orthodox than those of a certain church that I could mention. It is really rather surprising to see Christian doctrine expressed in a hymn, because it is a little hard to sing some of the doctrine, but it is there, and it is very clear.

MR. MORGAN: *What about the people themselves? Do they*

appear to be zombies or are they normal, or what are they like?

DR. GOETCHIUS: Well, they are certainly not zombies. I am not quite sure whether normal is a pejorative term or not. But I was proud to have them in my house; I am proud to have them as friends. Many people would not describe me as normal, but I like them, and they seem to like me.

MR. MORGAN: *Did they have some air of exclusiveness about them, or were you allowed to join with them?*

DR. GOETCHIUS: They certainly did not have any air of exclusiveness. My children were also there. My children are fairly obtrusive because they take after me, and we all enjoyed each other.

MR. MORGAN: *Finally, the pray-reading. Have you observed that?*

DR. GOETCHIUS: I have. I have taken part in it. Because I was Episcopalian and not a Catholic—so I am just one step removed—it was hard, but this was one thing that put me off a little bit. But I find from research about them that this is not just a tradition in the Eastern Church, but the German Pietists practiced something like this, using the Bible to pray. I think that is probably where the tradition would come from.

In any case, it certainly is not a mantra. This is something which has meaning, and in fact the purpose of the pray-reading is really to digest the Word. That is the way I understand it. You are praying in the words of Scripture, which is the way both your missal and our prayer book are made. They are made in words of Scripture.

MR. MORGAN: *Did you see any evidence that when they pray-read they hyperventilated, and they got in an altered state of consciousness where somebody could impose their will on them?*

DR. GOETCHIUS: No, and there wasn't anybody to impose their will on, for that matter. This was at a house, and everyone exchanged opinions and prayed together openly and freely. There wasn't a visible leader to this.

MR. MORGAN: *Have you attended any "Local Church" functions?*

DR. GOETCHIUS: Yes. Two or three weeks ago I went to the

dedication of the new meeting hall at the church in Newton where the children of the Sunday school gave their little skits, like many other places.

The mayor of Newton was there, the mayor of Newton happens to be Jewish. He knew a number of the members of the leadership of the "Local Church" there by first name. He gave the leader a yarmulke, which was accepted amid laughter, and it was a very fine occasion.

The children acquitted themselves beautifully. My wife borrowed the tape of the meeting so she could get the music, though not the words, for the songs and take to the school where she teaches. It was designed for the children. The children were beautifully behaved. I saw one child crying, and that was because she had stepped on a nail.

MR. MORGAN: *Are you describing, Reverend, then, a group of people that appear to be above normal in intelligence and in the manner in which they comport themselves?*

DR. GOETCHIUS: Well, they certainly were—I don't know what you mean by above normal, but this was a very pleasant group of people to be in.

I was invited, so it was clear they weren't that exclusive. My wife was invited. The mayor of Newton was invited. One of the members of my Greek class whom I know best of all, he was the original go-between for me and the group in Anaheim, his sister was present. His sister is an ordained Methodist minister, so obviously his family has not been broken by this. He has lovely children. The children are in many ways the most impressive thing about the church, I think, to me.

MR. MORGAN: *Does that mirror something of the church?*

DR. GOETCHIUS: Yes, I think it mirrors the right kind of relationship between the adults and the children. It is the kind of thing that Witness Lee teaches, which is the kind of thing the Bible teaches.

He teaches a sort of subordination which is not terribly popular in some circles today, but if you have everybody equal, you have sort of a riot, which is what one does have in some houses that I have visited. But this was an orderly and cheerful group of people who—I wouldn't say they knew their place–but they had a place which belonged to them, and this was their place, and they liked it, and they were respected for being what they were.

MR. MORGAN: *Thank you, I have nothing further.*
JUDGE SEYRANIAN: *Thank you very much.*

EDITORS NOTE: *Dr. Goetchius signed the following statement. Although it was not made a part of the court transcript, we include it here as a confirmation to his testimony.*

A little over a year and a half ago I was approached by a group of young people who asked me to give them a course in New Testament Greek. Rather hesitantly I suggested that they could enroll in a regular course I was already giving four days a week in the mornings. (I was hesitant because their number would make the class rather unwieldy.) Their own business commitments, however, made a regular morning class impossible. (They were, I later discovered, almost all computer "specialists" of one sort or another.) They asked me if I would give them a class in the evening. I was really loth to do this, so to discourage them I named what I thought would be an exorbitant fee. To my surprise they agreed to this at once, so I had to give up my Friday evenings—from 7:30 to 9:30—for the whole fall semester.

The first class was another surprise: I have been accustomed to begin a semester of classes with an opening prayer (since my courses are, after all, somewhat theological in nature), and I did so that evening in September 1983. Episcopalians are supposed to respond to a prayer with "Amen," and most of them do, albeit very lamely in many cases. My new students, however, responded heartily, even enthusiastically, not only with "Amen!" but with "Praise the Lord!" and even "Hallelujah!" I confess I was a little disconcerted (Episcopalians are sometimes, not without reason, called "God's frozen people"), but I began the class and continued to meet these students regularly once a week for one semester, then every two weeks for two more semesters.

These young men (and one young woman) informed me that they were members of the Church in Newton—the "Local Church". I had never heard of the Local Churches, and, at that time, I made no particular effort to find out more about them. What was quite obvious to me, however, was that these were young people—in their twenties and early thirties—of above average ability and intelligence, well motivated in the study of Greek. Meeting two hours a week they covered as much as my regular classes meeting four hours a week; to say the least, they were in no way inferior to my regular students.

I expressed interest one evening in learning more about the Local Churches. I was given a small book by Witness Lee, from which I learned, among other things, that Lee was an associate and follower of Watchman Nee, whose own book, *The Normal Christian Life,* had been presented to me a year or so earlier by one of my Episcopalian students, and which I had read with approval and great profit to myself. Witness Lee himself came to visit in the Church in Newton not long after this, and my class invited me to come hear him. This I did, and was privileged to hear a remarkably clear and concise exposition of almost the whole New Testament! Witness Lee's lecture was rather longer than those I am accustomed to enjoy (or even tolerate), but he held my attention without difficulty. I found Witness Lee's interpretation of the Scripture rather more conservative—perhaps traditional would be a better word—than I would myself present, but it certainly had no unusual features. To the best of my recollection Witness Lee said nothing on that occasion which could not have been endorsed by a good many Biblical scholars of my acquaintance who teach at impeccably respectable colleges, universities, and seminaries, and who belong to organizations such as the Society of Biblical Literature and the Studiorum Novi Testamenti Societas. I spoke briefly to Witness Lee on that occasion and was cordially welcomed.

Later in that first semester my wife and I were entertained at dinner by the students in my Greek class; the dinner was at the church's administrative and educational center, and the wives and children of my students were also present. Dinner was of the "potluck" type, and the luck was excellent and ample. Grace before dinner was more protracted and enthusiastic than Episcopalians are used to, but the really impressive thing to me was the behavior of the children—quite young, most of them, but one and all were almost miraculously civilized. By this I do not mean repressed—they were full of life, but they were also polite. "Miss Manners" would approve of them all.

Near the end of my second semester of teaching Greek to these Local Churchmen, my wife and I invited them and their families to spend the day with us at our house on Cape Cod. The weather was not especially good so we had to stay in the house most of the day, and there were a great many children. But there were no problems. No child sulked or whined. We enjoyed good conversation together, and finally we sat around and sang several hymns. These were not Episcopalian hymns, but Local Church hymns—many of which were composed by Witness Lee. These were rendered lustily by all, including myself. I was later presented with a copy of their hymnal: if anyone doubts the orthodoxy of the Local Churches, let them inspect their hymnal! Many of its hymns are doctrinally much sounder than some I could mention from the official hymnal of my own Church.

It was after embarking on a third semester of Greek study with the members of the Local Church that I came across a copy of a book called *The God-Men*. In it the Local Churches are accused of holding heretical doctrines and indulging in immoral practices—the sort of things that "main-line" Christians like myself would regard as characteristic of the religious lunatic fringe and especially of certain of the "cults" which seem to have a kind of hypnotic attraction for many young people, leading them to abandon their families and friends. I am exceedingly thankful that I did not read this book before I met the members of the Church in Newton who studied Greek with me! If I had read it first, I might have believed it, since I had no other experience of the Local Churches, and since, like other fathers of teenage children, I have become very anxious at the thought of the word "cult." Having met "real, live" members of the Local Church, however, having taught them, having discussed the New Testament passages with them, having been entertained by them and having entertained them in my home—after all this, of course I knew the book's thesis was absurd.

A book like *The God-Men* would have no readers if the Local Churches and their teachings were more widely known. The Episcopal Church, in which I am an ordained priest, is regarded with suspicion by some people, and I have actually read of a young person who, having become an Episcopalian against the wishes of his family, was "deprogrammed" at their behest. Few people would conclude from this that the Episcopal Church is a "cult", or that association with Episcopalians is dangerous: we have all known too many "real, live" Episcopalians, most of whom are not only not dangerous but not even very interesting. We could not be misled by a scurrilous attack on Episcopalians, Presbyterians, Methodists, or Roman Catholics: we know too many of them "in the flesh" to be fooled into believing that any of them are, *as a group*, evil, malicious, or specially misguided. The Local Churches, however, are, so to speak, "sitting ducks" for an attack such as is found in *The God-Men:* few people know many members of the Local Churches, so they are more likely to be misled by a book purporting to be an analysis and critique of Local Church doctrine and conduct.

I shared my low opinion of *The God-Men* with my Local Church Greek students; as a result I was visited shortly afterward by members of some of the Local Churches in California, who asked me to undertake a detailed examination of the charges in *The God-Men*. I agreed to do this because I was convinced, on the basis of my personal acquaintance and friendship with members of the Church in Newton, that the allegations made in *The God-Men* were unfounded. I felt qualified to do this because I have been a teacher of New Testament interpretation and exegesis for nearly thirty years, having taught Episcopalian students in my own seminary, Jesuit students from the Weston School of Theology, and students from the Harvard Divinity School. I have lectured in courses taught jointly with Roman Catholic and Lutheran scholars. I fancied, therefore, that I might have some idea of normative Christian faith and practice.

I re-read *The God-Men* and even dipped into the German

edition of this work (the latter contains a reference to the "Reverend" Jim Jones and his "People's Temple"; readers could naturally infer that the Local Churches are comparable to this misguided leader's ill-fated "family" who committed mass suicide in South America). I read several of Witness Lee's books, especially those that are most frequently quoted in *The God-Men* (*The Practical Expression of the Church, The Vision of God's Building, The Experience of Life, The All-Inclusive Christ, The Economy of God, The Knowledge of Life,* and *How to Meet*). I read a careful doctrinal statement entitled *The Testimony of Church History Regarding the Mystery of the Mingling of God with Man*, by William Freeman (a member of the Local Church); the book contains a commendatory preface by Professor G. D. Bromiley, an eminent scholar of impeccable orthodoxy. I read a booklet succinctly entitled, *The Beliefs and Practices of the Local Churches;* the authors of *The God-Men* would have done well to give it more attention.

The God-Men contains enough true statements to make it doubly misleading, because the statements are taken out of context or represented as illustrative of doctrines which are peculiar to the Local Churches. Thus, for example, the book states (and intimates in its very title) that the Local Churches teach the "mingling" of God with man; so they do: but so did many early Church Fathers, including St. Athanasius the Great—without whom we might not have the Nicene Creed—and also, of course, the Evangelist St. John ("The Word became flesh" [1:14]; "In that day you will know that I am in my Father, and you in me, and I in you" [14:20]). Nowhere do I find Witness Lee teaching that human beings can "become" God Almighty; such a doctrine is embraced in some religions, but Christianity is not one of them.

The book criticizes Witness Lee for "systematically" disparaging "the Law" (p. 37), but it fails to mention that in doing this Witness Lee is following in the footsteps of St. Paul (read Galatians and Romans, if you doubt this). The book criticizes the moral standards of the members of the Local Churches, calling them "moral pygmies" (p. 76). This criticism is utterly baseless: I know too many members of the Local Churches too well; their moral standards are well above those of "conventional" morality. Indeed, I am certain that my own Episcopalian students would regard members of the Local Churches as rather "square". They are not this, either; those I have met are "clean cut" and dress somewhat conservatively by some standards, but everyone of them that I am aquainted with possesses a well-developed sense of humor—surely not a characteristic of "cult" members.

One very significant criticism of the Local Churches is leveled at their doctrine of "locality", that is, the teaching that there can be only one church in each city. This teaching does, of course, have New Testament warrant: there was only one church in Corinth, one in Philippi, and so on. But in insisting on it today might seem to "unchurch" many Christians in other bodies, and, in fact, the Local Churches have been accused of exclusivism. It is nevertheless true that any Christian who wishes to worship with the Local Churches is welcome even to receive communion—which is certainly not true in the case of many older established denominations. I myself was certainly accepted without hesitation, and Witness Lee himself has addressed me as "brother" both in person and in a letter. The "locality" teaching does have real value, however, for every ecumenically inclined Christian will admit that there *ought* to be only one church in each city—not a single congregation, perhaps, for that could be unwieldy—but one body of Christians sharing one hope and one faith and one Lord, one God (cf. Ephesians 4:4f). The Local Churches may seem to be, and may develop into, "just another denomination"; but their doctrine of "locality" makes them a witness to a genuine Christian ideal: the unity of Christendom.

I have more recently met members of other Local Churches besides the Church in Newton, Massachusetts. I have attended meetings in their meeting halls and meetings in their homes. The members I encountered in these meetings were drawn from every age-group and from every race: all received me cordially and accepted me as a brother. Just last week I attended a meeting of the Church in Newton during which they celebrated the completion of their new meeting hall—a building built almost entirely by the members. The

Mayor of Newton (who happens to be Jewish) was present: he congratulated them on their achievement and welcomed their presence as valuable citizens. Doubtless he had not read *The God-Men:* he did, however, know a number of the members of the Church in Newton personally, for he called them by their first names. Also at this meeting was a sister of one of my Local Church Greek students: she is an ordained minister in the Methodist Church. She is not alienated from her brother. The Local Church does not "break up" families, as has been alleged. If my own children were to join one of the Local Churches I would not be dismayed, nor would I feel that I had been "abandoned" or "rejected"—and I would certainly have no cause to abandon or reject them.

One more thing; what about the "enthusiasm" of the Local Churches, which struck me as strange and which is so unlike the staid and "proper" behavior of the "main-line" denominations? Why do the members of the Local Churches shout "Amen!" and "Hallelujah!" and "Praise the Lord!" when Witness Lee proclaims, "God has saved us so that we may have His life. He has forgiven our sins. He has cleansed us. He has sanctified us. He has justified us. He has set us free." Why do Witness Lee's hearers shout so joyfully? Well, perhaps they understand what he said, and believe it.

CHAPTER FIVE

THE TESTIMONY OF RODNEY STARK, Ph.D.

MR. MORGAN: *You are Dr. Stark, is that right?*
DR. STARK: Yes.
MR. MORGAN: *What is your occupation or calling?*
DR. STARK: I am Professor of Sociology and Comparative Religion at the University of Washington.
(Curriculum vitae dated August 1983 of Rodney Stark marked for identification as plaintiff Exhibit 22.)
MR. MORGAN: *Let me show you what's been marked as Exhibit 22, and I will ask you to identify that document.*
DR. STARK: Yes, it is my vitae.
MR. MORGAN: *How current is your vitae?*
DR. STARK: Well, this is 1983. I guess there's been another book, and I suppose far too many articles.
    MR. MORGAN: *I will offer that into evidence at this time, Your Honor.*
    JUDGE SEYRANIAN: *Be accepted.*
MR. MORGAN: *Do you want to tell us something about your education, where you went to college and what degrees you received?*
DR. STARK: I got a degree in journalism from the University of Denver, and I have an M.A. and a Ph.D. from the University of California at Berkeley.
MR. MORGAN: *And the Ph.D.?*
DR. STARK: Sociology.
MR. MORGAN: *Did you also have some experience in journalism?*
DR. STARK: Yes, I was a reporter for the *Oakland Tribune* and the *Denver Post*.
MR. MORGAN: *Can you tell us what years you did that?*

DR. STARK: The *Denver Post* in the middle fifties, and then I was in the army, and then I was at the *Oakland Tribune* in '59 and '60, and I think a little bit of '61. That was a very long time ago.

MR. MORGAN: *Then did you go to Berkeley?*

DR. STARK: Yes. Well, I started at the *Tribune,* and then after a year of that I started at Berkeley, and then I did both for awhile.

MR. MORGAN: *Do you have some particular specialty at the present time?*

DR. STARK: Yes, I would have to say that my specialty all along has pretty much been the sociology of religion with particular emphasis, say, in the last period in religious movements.

MR. MORGAN: *Can you tell the court generally what is the field of sociology of religion?*

DR. STARK: It is anything anybody wants to call it, but as opposed to historians, we are not so interested in a specific group over a long period of time as opposed to psychologists or anthropologists.

There are many things. What is the effect of religion on crime rates, for example, would be a perfectly appropriate set of topics. What is the nature of religious movements, how do they recruit, how do they form, how do they grow, what separates the winners from the losers. That would also be the sociology of religion. What is the implication of Protestantism on the rise of industrialization in western Europe is another classic area, so it goes all over the map.

MR. MORGAN: *You have indicated that you were in 1982 and 1983 the president for the Association for the Sociology of Religion. Can you tell the court something about that organization, what it is?*

DR. STARK: Well, it is an international scholarly society made up of people who are sociologists in religion.

MR. MORGAN: *As president, is that an elective office?*

DR. STARK: That is an elective office, and it is largely ceremonial and honorific.

MR. MORGAN: *Then you have listed a number of pages of books and articles. I won't go into those, but I gather that you have written constantly, is that correct?*

DR. STARK: It is my disease.

MR. MORGAN: *Were you requested to make an evaluation for me of the "Local Church," its people, and the publications by SCP and Mr. Duddy?*

DR. STARK: Yes, I was.

MR. MORGAN: *Can you tell the court what you did in that regard? Were you also asked to do something else? Were you asked to review something in the book regarding the use of your name?*

DR. STARK: Yes, I was asked to read some pages, which didn't take very long, that purported to explicate something that I have gotten some, I guess, notoriety or whatever for. It is a theory of conversion that's been around for twenty years, and I was asked to see if Duddy had reported it correctly and applied it appropriately.

MR. MORGAN: *We will get to it again later, but what was your conclusion?*

DR. STARK: If a student had ever given me that, a freshman, I'd have flunked him.

MR. MORGAN: *Tell the court what you did by way of study of the "Local Church" and review of the publications.*

DR. STARK: Well, to a much less extent than some of the earlier witnesses, I have gone out and met members. I have attended some services. I have been in the Freeman home. I have seen the headquarters in Seattle. I have looked at a lot of TV tape. I have read or read parts of a substantial number of publications by Witness Lee.

MR. MORGAN: *Let me go now to the publication. Does* The God-Men *purport to be a sociological study of the "Local Church"?*

DR. STARK: Yes, it does. It says specifically in the very beginning of the book that it has two basic strands that it is going to evaluate: on religious grounds and on sociological grounds.

MR. MORGAN: *Can you comment for the court your opinion as to the merit of the sociological study?*

DR. STARK: It has none.

MR. MORGAN: *Can you tell us why it has none?*

DR. STARK: Well, first of all, there is not the slightest effort to have given it any. As was said earlier today, there is no methodology; there is no social science here. No one collected any data. No one tried to formulate any testable hypotheses and see if they were confirmed vis-à-vis what goes on in the "Local Church." There isn't a shred of sociology to it. There is the invoking of some sociological trappings.

MR. MORGAN: *Are there some accepted methods of sociological study of religious movements?*

DR. STARK: There are a varied number of them, I suppose. One could, for example, go out and do some observation. One could go out and hang around a group, be with a group, watch them.

So when John Lofland and I did research, for example, on the basis of the conversion theory, we went out and found a group in San Francisco, and we spent a couple of years, Lofland more than I. We spent a large amount of our time with those people, watching people actually join religious movements.

It is all well and good to sit in a library and speculate about who might have been attracted, but the only way you can find out who would be attracted is to go and see who is attracted and who comes in and fools around and nibbles a little bit and says no and goes away. That is the only way it can be done.

One could, of course, having some reasonably well-fashioned notions, give people questionnaires. This could be done very usefully.

For example, Eileen Barker at the London School of Economics has for many years now been giving questionnaires to all people who show up in London at the first workshop, say, of a Unification Church, the Moonies. They let her do it. The people fill them out. She's now got data going ten, twelve years. In the long run she knows who actually joins the church, who stayed, and when they quit. That is science. That is social science. There is none of that here.

MR. MORGAN: *Let me ask you, would it be social science to talk to three, four, five ex-members and then use that as your basis?*
DR. STARK: Well, we don't have to talk social science, that wouldn't be journalism.
MR. MORGAN: *Why not?*
DR. STARK: My city editor at the *Oakland Tribune* would have canned me for something like that. Let's get religion out of here.

Let's say he says, "Why don't you go out to Cal, and see how the Sigma Chi are doing." I go out to Cal, but I can't find any, but I can find three guys that de-pledged for whatever reason. Maybe they were cuckoo. I go interview these guys about Sigma Chi at Cal, and they tell me they are a bunch of bums and this, that, and the other thing.

What do I know? I don't know anything that I can trust. The best way, I suppose, would be to walk in the Sig house, give them the secret handshake, and hang around for a few months or whatever.

I took this out of religious context intentionally because what would you say about interviewing five guys who had gotten disbarred in Alameda County about the Alameda County Bar Association. Or say they hadn't gotten disbarred; let's say they had gotten disgruntled and had gone to be chiropractors. That is not the way you go about these things.

MR. MORGAN: *Let me ask you to refer to* The God-Men's *use of the phrase, "The Seduction Syndrome." Is that a sociological term?*
DR. STARK: I had never seen it before, until I was given a copy of *The God-Men* to look at.
MR. MORGAN: *First it mentions Dr. Anthony Campolo. Who is he?*
DR. STARK: I have no idea.
MR. MORGAN: *Then Duddy goes on; he says*:

> *Dr. Anthony Campolo, an evangelical Christian sociologist who teaches at the University of Pennsylvania, has done exceptional research on the topic of cultic religious conversions. He endorses the Lofland-Stark model of conversion as a useful*

basis for understanding conversion from natal beliefs to a deviant religion.

Lofland-Stark, does that ring a bell?

DR. STARK: Yes, that is John Lofland and Rodney Stark, "Becoming a World-Saver: A Theory of Conversion to a Deviant Perspective," *American Sociological Review of 1965.* We were young; we had much to learn, but we broke new ground then. So everything kind of seems to go back to this stuff, although I must say there are 1980 versions of this thing that are a whole lot less antique but, yes, I do recognize this.

MR. MORGAN: *For the benefit of some of us, what is a model? What are we talking about?*

DR. STARK: A theory in which we lay out some variables or some steps or some conditions or set of propositions trying to explain how it is that people go from A to B.

In this case we are talking about how is it that people ever decided to take up a new religious belief system which is quite different, say, than why a person in a Christian tradition, raised as a Christian, suddenly gets much more committed to his Christianity and talks about having a conversion.

I am talking about what happened to Paul. He was a Jew one minute, and he was a Christian the next minute. We are talking about a shift in perspective. What we attempted to do was to explain how this occurred.

MR. MORGAN: *Also Mr. Duddy writes:*

> Other prominent sociologists in accord with Campolo include William Bainbridge of the University of Washington.

Do you know William Bainbridge?

DR. STARK: I have published about twenty-five papers with him and I guess the third book is on the way, so, yes, I have written with the man quite a lot.

MR. MORGAN: *In your opinion, would Mr. Bainbridge approve of Mr. Duddy's utilization of the Lofland-Stark Model here?*

DR. STARK: He would throw up.

MR. MORGAN: *Mr. Duddy goes on, then, to in effect restate your model. Does he accurately restate it?*

Dr. Stark: No. He does not. He misses the entire point.

Mr. Morgan: *Maybe I could ask you first to tell the court in substance what Mr. Duddy says is your model.*

Dr. Stark: The model basically has two sets of elements. We could call them background elements and process elements.

The background elements are characteristics of individuals that they develop over time or they were born with. These are the characteristics people bring with them to the situation in which they encounter either family and friends who have suddenly taken up a new religious outlook or they run into people who are out there with a new religious outlook, new in terms of their background.

These people could be Baptists or they could be Moonies, but different from your previous background. All right. So there are those aspects. Those are the aspects the social science had always concentrated on.

Well, these people must be feeling a little antsy, to the extent that they aren't perfectly satisfied with their religion. They must probably not be complete atheists if you are going to try and convert them to religion. If they absolutely cannot accept the conceivable, that there is a spiritual world, presumably there are some background beliefs that lock people off from the possibility of changing. Somebody who is a very satisfied Catholic doesn't become something different.

So we isolated some of these conditions, and we get to a point where we are talking about a turning point in people's lives. I hate the language now. But what it really meant, and we spelled it out, is that people are structurally more or less available during the course of their lives.

When you are married and have a job and five kids, you have less freedom to conceive of a new kind of life. When you are nineteen years old and just came to San Francisco from Biloxi, Mississippi, and you are looking for a job, you have got a lot of options open. You still don't know what you are going to be when you grow up, and you haven't got a wife and kids. People who are in that condition of freedom often find it much easier to shift who they are and what they are going to be when they grow up.

But up to this point we are talking pretty conventional social science, and we are kind of saying it is not important because there are millions and millions of people out there who meet all of these conditions and yet very few of them ended up joining the particular group we were looking at. And so at this point we introduced what we thought was the guts of the model, which is a process of interaction between the potential convert, if you will, and the group to be converted to. It is at this point that the door comes down, Duddy stops reporting the model, and in other words, he skips everything important in the model and comes with some flat assertions that are completely, almost diabolically, the reverse of what the model says.

MR. MORGAN: *In your opinion, could Mr. Duddy just have misunderstood your model?*

DR. STARK: Well, it's possible he never read it. No, it is entirely possible that he got a third- or fourth-hand re-chew of the thing that other people have been grinding up and passing around. It becomes almost an oral tradition out there. I can't be in Mr. Duddy's mind, and Mr. Duddy has told me nothing. I don't know whether he actually went and consulted the paper or not.

MR. MORGAN: *But if he read it?*

DR. STARK: If he did, then one doesn't want to underestimate the capacity of idiocy. I am forced to conclude that if he did read the paper, this was malicious.

MR. MORGAN: *And how did he alter the model?*

DR. STARK: What Lofland and I say is, hey, the world has millions of people out here qualified to change religions, and they definitely do not do that because certain social processes and conditions are required for conversion to occur. To sum it up, you end up accepting the religious views of your closest associates, whether these are new associates or old associates.

Very frequently people join a new religion because their friends and relatives join it before them, and this spreads through pre-existing friendship nets and bonds, which is the way the real world works; we influence one another. The reason most of us don't steal is because we influence one another. We kind of keep each other straight, and what we discovered watching conversion is that if people had more and closer ties to the group than they had ties to people outside the group trying to pull them back, they joined, but if the equation worked out the other way, they didn't join. The marvelous thing is how unimportant frequently religion was in this whole process.

That people could, in fact, hang around a group, like them, maybe be relatives of them, friends with them, whatever, but be there in a long period of close association expressing little or no interest in the religion and no belief in it, and eventually having their interest kindled by the fact that their friends really did care and were committed, and finally building up to a point, saying, you know, it just came to me last night that I have been just kind of wasting my time and failing to see the truth, and suddenly comes the vision.

Then a lot of things can get recoded by these people saying, actually I was always interested in religion. In my observation, watching them, they typically weren't.

MR. MORGAN: *How did Duddy's differ?*

DR. STARK: What he says, first of all, is that it is like knocking passenger pigeons out of the trees at this point. He is talking at this point of how any experienced proselytizer can take these people right over:

> The fourth, final stage in the seduction syndrome is the turning point—a moment of transition, migration or uncertainty such as a change and/or failure in career or school, divorce, etc., that renders the pre-convert rootless, thereby susceptible to messianic figures/groups. If, through peculiar happenstance, persons in the fourth state (the turning point) of the seduction syndrome—

MR. MORGAN: *That is not your words, is it?*

DR. STARK: No, there are no such words. I mean, it is a word but—

> —meet a purveyor offering to solve their personal problems within the natal method of the pre-convert, a conversion inevitably results (barring a "fumble" by the group's repre-

sentative or leader). Conversion, say Lofland and Stark, can be readily achieved by skilled proselyters.

It is not so. If I said it, I was an idiot. I hope that I can do a better job pretending not to be.

MR. MORGAN: *You're saying, "It did not say that"?*

DR. STARK: It did not say that. It said the reverse! Still, conversion is very rare of people who have fulfilled all these stages of the model, gotten to the turning point. What we were trying to stress was that the world is full of people. How many nineteen year olds are there? There are millions. There are all kinds of people who have just gotten divorced, just changed to a new town, just gotten out of school, just flunked out of school, or whatever.

There are lots of people who are loose and available and who might not think that their religion satisfied. There are millions of them, but they don't join groups. In order to do this you have got to build bonds of friendship and trust and affection and concern and interest.

I will bet there's never been anybody show up to the door of the "Local Church" saying, "Got your tract, here I am. I am ready to join." I have never seen a conversion like that happen in my life.

MR. MORGAN: *Have you also made studies on what happens after the conversion? How many stay?*

DR. STARK: Well, I haven't done a lot of that, but there certainly has been a great deal done on that. That will vary. Frankly, the people who join liberal Protestant congregations don't stay because there is no cohesive group life to hold them there. The more affection that people give you, the more you feel good about being someplace and the more you want to stay there.

Now in terms of what you might call the really heavy-duty religious movement, that is asking tremendous commitment from you; I guess the heavier the request, the more frequently that there is turnover in membership.

Lots and lots of people go into these groups in which the turnover is very high. Eileen Barker, as I said, has been studying the Moonies for about twelve years in London.

For every hundred people who actually show up at a workshop, so it means they have been preselected for having some interest, for being willing to come, for knowing Moonies.

They have been exposed to the mind benders. Out of every one hundred who comes, only about three ever join the church. Boy, is that a bad mind control. And of those, about half quit within the first eighteen months. So it must be relatively easy to do.

Of those who leave, it is hard pickings to find that many disgruntled people. People say, hey, that seemed like the thing to do, and boy, have I got a lot of good, warm friendships there, but now I think it is time to go do something else. That is kind of an interesting rhetoric compared to what we're being quoted here. I have never met a skilled proselytizer. There might be some guy someplace who can just walk up and do that, but he is busy doing something else.

JUDGE SEYRANIAN: *Do you believe that with some of these people that are converted, there is a need in the person that the people doing the conversion are able to satisfy a need? For instance, I remember reading in* Helter Skelter *that Manson says, "These were your children that you discarded or couldn't relate to or couldn't get along with. They were left sitting on the corner of the streets, and I came along, and they were in need of love and friendship, and I just provided it for them, and they came along."*

DR. STARK: Yes, I think he used a phrase like they were set out like the garbage.

JUDGE SEYRANIAN: *He said, "I picked up your garbage."*

DR. STARK: There are people around desperately in need of a connection, and so sometimes conversion can happen pretty darn fast. I am more familiar with the Love Family in Seattle, which is now disbanded, than with Manson; this group doesn't have nearly the ugly characteristics. They were a halfway house for all the sick and crazy and lost kids. You could crash with them. Some people found it real snug and real comfortable and real good, and so they stayed.

One of the interesting things is that now these people

are approaching forty and have children; they're feeling so good about themselves that they decided not to do it anymore.

MR. MORGAN: *In the book Mr. Duddy is purporting to show that this was a sociological study, isn't that right?*

DR. STARK: Yes, of course he was. There was no reason to bring this in but to give it the trappings of science and say, "By the way, if the religion isn't bad enough, and I have pointed out all these terrible, terrible, terrible things of being unbiblical, let me tell you these people have been identified as part of this ugly crowd by scientific sociologists. They come and prey upon you and upon your children. I guess they can pray-read too, but it is a sinister image. They are standing at the alley with the net."

MR. MORGAN: *Immediately following this statement about the skilled proselytizer there is a story about a young girl named Cia who gets ensnared in this; is that right?*

DR. STARK: Yes, and as I recollect, the headline is that it is a case study. Well, a case study of what? I assumed that it was going to be some kind of effort to apply our model. It rambles away and doesn't with any great clarity do that, but it is clearly there. My stuff is used as a front end, as frosting on the cake for a horror story that he is now going to tell, and I gather when all is said and done, it was all hearsay.

MR. MORGAN: *And there is no support from your study for what he is saying, is there?*

DR. STARK: No.

MR. MORGAN: *Let me ask you this. You had a chance to study the "Local Church" people?*

DR. STARK: Well—

MR. MORGAN: *Not a sociological study.*

DR. STARK: I didn't sit on the couch with them or anything, but I saw and talked to them. Had very nice shortcake with them once. I needed it.

MR. MORGAN: *Let me ask you, can you give us your opinion as to where they fit in the spectrum of Christianity?*

DR. STARK: Well, being a sociologist of religion, I agree that Gordon Melton put them in the right volume of his book.

They are without a doubt an evangelical Protestant denomination. Given the kind of moral tone of the group, one would call them a sect rather than a church, a church being a place where the minister says, "Well, a spot of Jack Daniels is okay and let's go play golf," a sect saying, "Well, we don't need the golf course, and a 7-Up, please." They fit right in the middle of evangelical Protestantism. We never thought to classify them as anything else nor would any sociologist of religion that I would know of.

MR. MORGAN: *Are you saying they wouldn't be classified as a cult in the pejorative term?*

DR. STARK: Oh, pejorative or non-pejorative, I'm one of these idiots who clung to trying to use the word *cult* in a technical, sociological sense to mean a religious movement not in the main tradition of the society we are observing. So that Christianity is a cult movement in India; Hinduism is a cult movement in the United States.

I am now sorry I tried to fight this battle for twenty years because the newspapers have killed me. The newspapers are going to own that word, and it's going to mean awful, awfulness. It is going to mean Jim Jones. It is going to mean bad things.

But, going back to the word *cult* as a technical, useful word; it is precisely what I have said: no, absolutely not! Because we are not talking here about structure. We are talking about doctrine. Are they still within the conventional tradition within American society, and the answer is so obviously yes.

MR. MORGAN: *As a reporter you had a chance to review Duddy's work by way of investigative reporting. In your opinion, would you describe for us the type of investigative reporting that you saw he did in this book?*

DR. STARK: Well, I guess I have lost a lot of my faith in that old profession because the *National Enquirer* and lots of groups have come to the fore since then, but this isn't journalism. First of all, it is clear the book was written backwards.

MR. MORGAN: *What do you mean by that?*

DR. STARK: The conclusion is where the book starts, that the

Spiritual Counterfeits Project doesn't go after people to go out and say, "Hey—it isn't the Mobil four-star. We are going to give these people good ratings and these people bad ratings." They only write attacks. The decision had been made. There had been earlier rumbles over here, after all, by the same group. Duddy was given an assignment, and he did it.

Unfortunately, he didn't cover his tracks. He was extraordinarily careless, because as was clear in the depositions, he didn't check anything. If all he was going to do was write a book being real nasty to Witness Lee's theology, we wouldn't be here today, because that is fair in American society. You can do that.

But the second you start naming names and events, discrediting events, sexual hanky-panky, financial hanky-panky, or indeed getting to a certain point of quoting a man's theological statements diametrically opposed to what the man is saying, then I think we are not talking about religion; we are talking about truth; we are talking about libel; we are talking about fairness; we are talking about a whole constellation of things.

There is none of that here. This is the worst kind of rumormongering being passed off. But it is clear it was being done for a purpose, and it was systematic.

JUDGE SEYRANIAN: *Being what?*

DR. STARK: It was done for a purpose.

JUDGE SEYRANIAN: *Do you know what that purpose was?*

DR. STARK: Yes. For some reason, which I have no idea of, the "Local Church" was next on the hit list, and they got hit.

JUDGE SEYRANIAN: *I have a question. Do you feel that when you write books of this type that people would be more likely to read something negative than positive?*

DR. STARK: Sure. When I was at the *Oakland Tribune*, I can remember old Al Reck, rest his soul, sweet old city editor, jumping up and saying we have had a hell of a great air wreck.

JUDGE SEYRANIAN: *Obviously the volume of these books that are sold is nothing compared to any kind of a hit list book, so you are not going to make money on the number of books you sell, but does anything in your studies show that publishing these books where people would read them with this kind of a story would create contributions that might assist whatever you are trying to do in your cause, in other words, the writers of this book would seek to get additional contributions because people read these things and say, "Hey, these guys are real crusaders out here." Do you think that could occur in this kind of journalism?*

DR. STARK: Well, I think the motive for this kind of journalism is to damage the group as much as possible.

JUDGE SEYRANIAN: *Do you think people then contribute to these kind of things?*

DR. STARK: Oh, absolutely. I think that the project has been sold to a lot of people in the evangelical world as a good work, as a terribly important thing to help us guard our children, and you said the book doesn't have terrific circulation, but it can have very targeted circulation.

I met a young man. He had taken introductory sociology from me as a freshman. I didn't know that because I had eight hundred kids in the room. I met him. He's now become a member of the Local Church. When he was a student in my class and a freshman at the University of Washington, perhaps a sophomore, and had begun fellowshipping with the "Local Church" and was kind of checking it out, *The God-Men* was put on his bunk in his room in the dorm along with an anonymous note kind of suggesting that he ought to check out what he was playing around with because he was playing around with the devil, he was playing around with bad stuff. Here is a book published by what is thought to be a very legitimate—

MR. MORGAN: *Inter-Varsity Press.*

DR. STARK: Legitimate people. This is an evangelical kid, and so he is sensitive to the fact of anti-cult literature, if you will, and he didn't know. As it turns out, some of the people in the book were people he had already gotten to know, and he realized that it didn't wash.

But, sure, how many kids have been scared off? How many parents have been scared? The aim of this book is to keep the "Local Church" from converting the Christians to their particular denomination. That is the whole point. Spiritual Counterfeits is out there to warn. It is kind of a "consumer research" for the evangelical world as it is so conceived.

MR. MORGAN: *His Honor asked you, do you have any opinion that by SCP achieving this so-called fame that they in turn get assistance and contribution from people throughout the country?*

DR. STARK: I imagine that is a matter of public record since they are a nonprofit organization in bankruptcy.

JUDGE SEYRANIAN: *What would your opinion be?*

DR. STARK: Yes, of course. Let's put it this way. I could peddle this. I could raise funds.

MR. MORGAN: *Let me finish it now. What in your opinion has been the effect of this book, this manuscript on Witness Lee and the "Local Church"?*

DR. STARK: Well, I think it's been devastating, and I will give you as evidence an article in an extraordinarily influential publication a week or two ago called *Christianity Today*. It is the centerpiece of the evangelical world. They covered the fact that the trial didn't take place when it was supposed to, and the fact of the bankruptcy, and whatnot.

It was exceedingly unsympathetic, skirting very close structurally to some of the issues here with us today, and I am sure that these are not bad people sitting out there in Illinois. I think they are very misinformed people who still think that (A) *The God-Men* was right, it was an accurate book, and (B) the terrible problem that the evangelical world is facing, we are about to lose our "Consumer Guide," our consumer research agency, because these people are taking them to court and punishing them as an attempt to silence them.

That was the way this was reported, and I was prompted to write to the editor a long letter to try to clarify the moral issue of a day in court. But without the book, of course, there wouldn't have been the story. But without the book, I don't imagine that *Christianity Today* would be bothering much with the "Local Church" one way or the other. Gordon

Melton is one of the few people on earth who had heard of them in my world until this book came out, and Gordon Melton has heard of everyone.

MR. MORGAN: *Thank you. I have no further questions, Your Honor.*

JUDGE SEYRANIAN: *Thank you.*

Chapter Six

THE TESTIMONY OF H. NEWTON MALONY, Ph.D.

MR. MORGAN: *What is your business, profession, or calling?*
DR. MALONY: I'm a clinical psychologist.
MR. MORGAN: *All right. Let me show you what has been marked as Exhibit 23, and I will ask you if you can identify that?*
DR. MALONY: Yes. This is an abbreviated vitae plus my annual reports to my institution for the last three or four years. Basically, my updated vitae.
> MR. MORGAN: *I will offer that into evidence, Your Honor.*
> JUDGE SEYRANIAN: *It may be admitted.*
MR. MORGAN: *Let's talk a bit about your education. Would you tell the court where you went to college, when you graduated, what degrees you received, and what further education you have in that regard?*
DR. MALONY: I received an A.B. degree from Birmingham Southern College, Birmingham, Alabama, in 1952; a Master of Divinity degree from Yale Divinity School in 1955; a Master of Arts and Ph.D. in clinical psychology from George Peabody College of Vanderbilt University, 1961 and 1964; and I have done further study at the William Alanson White Institute of Psychiatry, Psychology, and Psychoanalysis, Emory University, Vanderbilt University, and Harvard University.
MR. MORGAN: *Now you have mentioned a divinity school?*
DR. MALONY: Yes.
MR. MORGAN: *Was there some purpose in going to divinity school?*
DR. MALONY: Yes. In addition to being a clinical psychologist, I'm an ordained United Methodist minister; I served as

parish pastor for over four years full-time, and part-time for eleven years; I was also chaplain during that time. I'm under appointment by my bishop in my present role.

MR. MORGAN: *And what is that role?*

DR. MALONY: I am Professor and Director of Programs in the integration of psychology and theology at Fuller Theological Seminary, Graduate School of Psychology.

MR. MORGAN: *Can you tell us basically what your field is that you have told us about, this integration of religion and psychology?*

DR. MALONY: I should preface what I have to say by saying that Fuller Seminary has three schools: Theology, World Missions, and School of Psychology where we train doctoral-level clinical psychologists who are Christian psychologists and who we hope are able to integrate their psychological knowledge with their theological expertise. Our students receive a masters in theology along the way toward their doctorate. And I direct the program that interfaces the two disciplines.

MR. MORGAN: *In addition, do you do teaching at Fuller?*

DR. MALONY: Yes.

MR. MORGAN: *Can you tell the court generally what courses you teach at Fuller?*

DR. MALONY: Having been there now sixteen years, I've taught across the curriculum. But over the last seven or eight years, this has narrowed down.

I teach the psychology of religion, I teach the integration of psychology and theology. I teach what are called topical integration courses on healing, conversion, behavior change, and conflict management. I teach courses on organizational management and church planning to the theology students every now and then. All sorts of courses. I teach clinical courses in such areas as consulting skills, psychodrama, management of clinical cases, transactional analysis, that sort of thing.

MR. MORGAN: *Are you ever engaged in the private practice of psychology?*

DR. MALONY: Yes, I have a private practice, up to ten hours a week, in which I counsel with adults, largely on individual matters. I do some marriage counseling, and then I consult with religious bodies and church organizations on a variety of matters having to do with organizational life.

MR. MORGAN: *All right. Doctor, is there some board, similar to the medical profession, where a person can be certified as a specialist in the field of Psychology?*

DR. MALONY: Yes. There are two levels of certification for clinical psychologists, both in the state and nationwide. One is licensure in a state. Psychology is a legal term in this state. You cannot call yourself a psychologist without being licensed. That requires a doctoral degree plus a minimum of one year supervised post-doctoral experience.

I've been licensed sixteen years and was previously licensed in the state of Tennessee. There is that first level of licensure, and then there is a subsequent optional level for which one may aspire. After a minimum of five years' experience, you can submit yourself to the American Board of Professional Psychologists to stand for their diplomat examination. I stood that examination in the early seventies and since 1972 have been a diplomat in clinical psychology under the American Board of Professional Psychology.

MR. MORGAN: *And have you also participated as an examiner of other diplomat candidates?*

DR. MALONY: I was the Chairman of the Western Regional Board of that board, have served on its national board, and have been an oral examiner here for the state licensing board exams which are held every year.

MR. MORGAN: *In addition to the activities you have outlined already, do you also contribute as an editor to various publications in your profession?*

DR. MALONY: Yes. My special area of research is the psychology of religion, so the journals on whose editorial boards I serve are all primarily related to that. For example, the *Journal of Psychology and Christianity,* the *Journal for the Scientific Study of Religion,* the *Review of Religious Research,* the *Journal of Psychology and Theology,* and the *Journal of the American Scientific Affiliation.*

MR. MORGAN: *In addition, Exhibit 23, your vitae, indicates you have written numerous other articles. Is that correct?*

DR. MALONY: Yes. And have either authored or edited, I think, thirteen books.

MR. MORGAN: Okay. Fine. Now let me ask you, you use the term "psychology of religion." What does that mean?

DR. MALONY: Well, the psychology of religion has been divided into two basic areas, one called functional psychology of religion; the second called substantive psychology of religion. William James, at the turn of the century, called this the study of *roots* on the one hand, which would be functional psychology of religion, why religion comes to be in persons' lives. Then he contrasted that with the *fruits* of religion, what people believe, how they behave, what it looks like out in the world. So that's briefly what the field is about, roots and fruits.

MR. MORGAN: *Okay. Great. Now, Doctor, were you requested on my behalf to make certain studies about Witness Lee and the "Local Church" as they relate to some publications by Neil Duddy and SCP?*

DR. MALONY: Yes. I assume as a result of a book which I co-authored several years ago, now entitled *Christian Conversion, Biblical and Psychological Perspectives* and also as a function of a book of readings called *Contemporary Perspectives in the Psychology of Religion.*

A representative of the "Local Church" approached me about entering in or serving you in that way, and I should say, personally, I had never heard of the "Local Church" before that. I may have heard of the Spiritual Counterfeits Projects. I don't remember. I knew nothing about the whole issue.

MR. MORGAN: *Okay. Would you tell the court what you understood your assignment to be on my behalf?*

DR. MALONY: First of all, to read the accusations made against the "Local Church" in, I guess, such books as the one in front of me, *The God-Men*. Then to undertake any endeavor to ascertain, in my opinion, the extent to which these accusations were well-founded, legitimate, and true.

MR. MORGAN: *Okay. Can you tell the court what, in your opinion, is the thrust of Exhibit 1, the manuscript, as it relates to Witness Lee and the "Local Churches"?*

DR. MALONY: The thrust was defamatory.

MR. MORGAN: *And can you tell us in what respect?*

DR. MALONY: It seemed to me to be an attempt to discredit both the contents or teachings of this group and their behavior and social practice.

MR. MORGAN: *All right. And in your opinion, did the book create any form of an image of both Witness Lee and the group?*

DR. MALONY: Without any question.

MR. MORGAN: *And what was that image?*

DR. MALONY: It was to associate this group with what was called an aberrant Christian group or, more specifically, by innuendo, to associate it with what would be in the common world "cults," common everyday language. And I basically assume that those groups that the public calls "cults" are going to be avoided.

MR. MORGAN: *All right. What is your understanding of the common definition of a cult today?*

DR. MALONY: I'm much more acquainted with the technical definition of a cult, but I can give you my impression of what people think of when they hear the word *cult*, as something resembling the church of Satan or Jim Jones or Charles Manson or Hari Krishnas or the Moonies, which I think are thought to be semi-secret, manipulative, non-Christian groups who are seducing the public in some way toward an evil end.

JUDGE SEYRANIAN: *Doctor, in the common language today, secret doesn't seem to be evil—you know the Masons are secret.*

DR. MALONY: And the Masons have been called a cult.

JUDGE SEYRANIAN: *Maybe they are in your definition. What I am trying to find out is, in our common understanding, is there anything that associates people and cults today with some form of mind-controlling, mind-influencing?*

DR. MALONY: Oh, yes, I think so.

JUDGE SEYRANIAN: *Is that part of your understanding today?*

DR. MALONY: It may not have been the terms. I think

the deviousness, the misrepresentation, or even the counter-cultural dimension of it.

JUDGE SEYRANIAN: *Well, let's say, for instance, we hear the term in this day and age which has been relatively new, "brainwashing." Would you, in this day and age, associate brainwashing with cults?*

DR. MALONY: I think that definitely the term brainwashing has become associated with cults, that they brainwash people against their will, against their better judgment, for ends that are not good.

JUDGE SEYRANIAN: *Does the average person, when he reads a story and it says, "This is a cult," does he associate it, in your opinion, to some form of religion that's mind-controlling, brainwashing, secret, some of the things that you have said?*

DR. MALONY: Yes, I don't think there is any question about it. I think, for example, not only in the general public but in the educated public from other fields of study. For example, I think that my colleagues who are not students of the psychology of religion or the sociology of religion, my colleagues perhaps in New Testament, or my colleagues in World Missions, if somebody was to say to them, such and such a group is a cult, those are the exact associations they would have.

JUDGE SEYRANIAN: *Okay.*

MR. MORGAN: *Now will you tell us what you did to carry out the assignment that we requested of you? What I would like you to do is to go through, just in general terms, the various things you did in order to assist you in formulating certain opinions.*

DR. MALONY: First of all, I asked for materials, both this manuscript and other materials, that might help me. And I was provided with depositions that had been taken from, I guess, expert witnesses or other people in this issue. I asked for writings of Witness Lee and for the writings of the church, and I was provided more than a human being could read.

Then I asked for addresses of "Local Churches" in the Los Angeles area where I might attend firsthand. I attended worship or training meetings in Anaheim, Fullerton, Temple City, and El Monte. On three of those occasions, I went unannounced, simply knowing the hours of meeting. On two other occasions, I went because I was invited to the training to hear Witness Lee.

I heard Witness Lee give two training addresses, I attended pray-reading sessions, and I attended Sunday morning meetings of the group. I also viewed videotapes of contemporary meetings within the last year, plus videotapes of meetings that were associated with the accusations against the "Local Church." I attended two depositions that were taken in this trial of expert witnesses. Then I undertook a survey to better acquaint myself with what was going on.

MR. MORGAN: *Does that cover pretty well what you did in this regard?*

DR. MALONY: I talked with a number of persons, leaders of the church.

MR. MORGAN: *Now after doing all that work, did you form some basic opinions regarding the charges or allegations that are in Exhibit 1?*

DR. MALONY: I did.

MR. MORGAN: *Based upon your opinion, what did you see as the basic charges that were being made in Exhibit 1, when you read it, as it relates to Witness Lee and the "Local Church"?*

DR. MALONY: I saw them to be of two types: beliefs and practices. I saw my charge to be that of functioning as a clinical psychologist, with background in the psychology of religious groups, to evaluate the practices.

MR. MORGAN: *All right. Fine. And what did you see were the defamatory charges of the practices in Exhibit 1?*

DR. MALONY: I believe they were three basic types: one, having to do with recruitment practices under the general rubric of a "seduction syndrome;" two, having to do with worship practices under the general rubric of brainwashing; and three, having to do with what I will call maintenance practices, how you keep people in the organization, under the rubric of coercion.

MR. MORGAN: *Let's take the first one, the recruitment, the "seduction syndrome." First, is that an accepted professional term "seduction syndrome"?*

DR. MALONY: No, that is a term coined by the author of this book.

MR. MORGAN: *Okay. What do you understand the author intends to convey to the reader by the term "seduction syndrome"?*

DR. MALONY: That the recruitment practices of the "Local Church" were qualitatively different and bad and evil, qualitatively different from those recruitment practices of other religious groups.

MR. MORGAN: *In your opinion, having done all the work you have related, is there any validity in that charge?*

DR. MALONY: I do not think there is any validity to that charge.

MR. MORGAN: *Okay. Let's go to the next one, worship, and you said it was under the rubric of brainwashing?*

DR. MALONY: Yes.

MR. MORGAN: *Did you form any opinion as to whether there is any validity to that charge?*

DR. MALONY: Yes.

MR. MORGAN: *What is your opinion?*

DR. MALONY: There is no validity to that charge.

MR. MORGAN: *Then the last one was the general field of maintenance or, namely, coercion. Are you saying coercion in keeping the people?*

DR. MALONY: In line and in their organization.

MR. MORGAN: *All right. Did you form any opinion as to whether there was any validity to that charge?*

DR. MALONY: I felt there was no validity.

MR. MORGAN: *Okay. Now we'll go back to them. First, let's talk about the so-called "seduction syndrome" that the defendants have coined. What do you understand that the writers are saying the church is doing in this regard?*

DR. MALONY: I understand that the writers are saying that the church follows a pattern of preying on the weak and then seducing them against their knowledge or will by a process of seduction. The very phrase of seduction means to me that something is done by the use of one dynamic for another purpose.

MR. MORGAN: *All right. And what you have told us now is that in your opinion, that it's not true as it relates to either Witness Lee or the "Local Church." Is that right?*

DR. MALONY: Yes.

MR. MORGAN: *Now will you explain to the court why, in your opinion, you feel that is not a true statement?*

DR. MALONY: Let me begin by saying that I think that the writer of the book misused a scholarly article in this regard, the Lofland and Stark model of "conversion to a deviant perspective," which is now over a decade old. It was intended to say one thing, but the author of this volume misconstrued it to say another thing, and then applied that to the "Local Church." There is an interesting issue here.

The Lofland and Stark Model, called a problem-solving model, presumes that an individual is in the time of stress and that they somehow are then met by another individual with a simplistic solution to their problem and that then they are swept off their feet and only discover later, if ever, that they have been duped.

That was not the intent of the original article itself, nor has it become the obvious implications of this model in a number of scholarly articles written since that time. I'll explain what I mean.

The Lofland and Stark article assumed that persons who are converted are under stress, trying to settle a problem in their lives. That is what we might call an accidental event in their lives, their parents have died, they failed a course, ad infinitum, something you wouldn't expect in the developmental process.

Later events have reconfirmed what we have known to be true for seventy years, since the early study of William James and his students at Harvard. Conversion is predominantly an adolescent phase of life experience. Many of the persons that Lofland and Stark thought of as experiencing problems are really seeking purpose or meaning to their lives, quite normally, and the social institutions that they were involved with in their earlier years may or may not meet those needs. So transferring one's loyalty to another group, another social institution, is much more a normal late-adolescent phase of the life problem than the author of this book makes it out to be.

I can only presume that the author didn't know developmental psychology or has had limited religious experience. Charles Stewart, for example, writing from the Menninger Foundation on adolescent religion, says there is one of three ways that adolescents may react to their former religious background. Quite normally, they may leave it entirely, which a number of adolescents do. That's been a documented sociological phenomenon, that people leave religion in late adolescence. Secondly, those who leave but return to it in mid-life. Thirdly, those who conform to their religious upbringing, go right on with it, and become ardent members of it.

I've seen that in my parish, where certain churches were characterized by parents and their children as proselytizers. Or they may take an alternative route that has similarities or dissimilarities to their parent's religion.

Melton and Moore, for example, writing in *The Cult Experience,* see this as very normal and as very natural. And they say, for example, that most people leave the cults after two or three years. I don't think that's been necessarily true of the "Local Church." People find their homes there. It's much more the similar type to their parents' religion.

MR. MORGAN: *Then are you saying that even the first premise that the author of this book was utilizing, namely, that the people are walking around wounded, is not a scientific basis that's been accepted by the professions?*

DR. MALONY: That's right. I'd also like to say that it's much more a natural social process, not a deviant one.

For example, I wonder if the author of this book has read any evangelistic theory. I understand the author had seminary training at Westminster. But one wonders, did he ever take an evangelism course? Some of these processes are taught as natural conversion overtures in most evangelistic courses. Church growth theory, which is a very important theory at my seminary, even makes the point that, if you are wanting your church to grow, you approach the people, the transients, that have just moved. If you want your church to grow, approach people who are in times of stress. Meet their needs.

Another interesting implication in the way this author describes the whole process is to suggest that religion offers simplistic, immediate answers to hard problems. Well, I think Christians, from the time of Jesus to the present, would say, Praise the Lord. That's true. That's what religion does.

MR. MORGAN: *I think His Honor has a question.*

JUDGE SEYRANIAN: *Professor, sticking to your first point, "seduction syndrome," I understand—maybe you recall this in the book, there was some place where the author says this religion is anti-sports, and there seems to be some exception to tennis playing. I don't understand why that comes in there, but they are contrary to sports. Now would you feel maybe, perhaps, that what the author is trying to convey is that taking these things away from people, such as normal activities like sports activities, gives more time in the church, that this would then hold them closer to the church? Is that the inference that is being made by that connotation?*

DR. MALONY: That's the inference.

JUDGE SEYRANIAN: *Could that be inferred normally from a layperson reading the book?*

DR. MALONY: Yes, in the sense that it is correlated also with not watching television and not being a part of the culture or not spending your time reading other than religious documents. But let me qualify it in two ways.

MR. MORGAN: *First, he wants to know what the book portrays.*

JUDGE SEYRANIAN: *Is that what the book would portray to the average person reading it?*

DR. MALONY: Yes. And they would say, "That is bad. That is evil."

JUDGE SEYRANIAN: *Now do you know from your experience in your investigative processes whether you found out that statement is true or not with respect to the principles and tenets of this religion?*

DR. MALONY: I found it not to be true from the survey that I did.

JUDGE SEYRANIAN: *I mean that statement about the fact that they discourage sports and TV watching; that is not a true statement?*

DR. MALONY: I think you are going to be provided in a minute with the questions I did ask. I didn't ask sports, but I asked the question, "Was the reading of newspapers, looking at TV, or listening to the radio discouraged? The uniform answer was, "No."

JUDGE SEYRANIAN: *But you didn't ask about this business about sports? In other words, would this church discourage people from participating in sports activities?*

Again, this is what the book is saying. I'm asking you whether you did anything to verify whether that statement is true or not with respect to this church. This may be going beyond what you were assigned to do, but I was curious to know.

DR. MALONY: No, but I would respectfully submit to Your Honor, I don't know what the statistics are on the percentage of the American population that participates in sports. I don't see participating in sports as a big deal one way or the other. I'm gathering you do.

JUDGE SEYRANIAN: *Maybe because I'm a sports lawyer. You are right about that. But I'm thinking now to the average layperson or someone reading this book, and what I am trying to find out is, do you believe in your experience, that if a church does discourage sports activities on the grounds that you will give more time to spend in more higher things, such as your church and your religion—would you think that would go into what we call the "seduction syndrome," holding you to the religion?*

DR. MALONY: As read by the average person, would the average person say, oh, that's bad?

JUDGE SEYRANIAN: *Yes.*

DR. MALONY: I think the average secular person would.

JUDGE SEYRANIAN: *Let's take you, for instance. Would*

you, as an expert, feel that if a church discourages sports activities, for instance, this is the one thing I'm just pointing out, and/or TV watching, for instance, and says to do so takes you away from the time that you can spend in your religion. And this is where your time should be spent. Do you feel, in your opinion, that is a form of seductive holding or seductive syndrome?

DR. MALONY: No. But let me qualify that. I don't use the term "seductive syndrome." And my experience seems to have been broad enough in my life to say that I have met many churches. I know churches who will not have a baseball team or not have a softball team, and it's not simply the "Local Church." I don't know whether they have softball teams or not, but they will do it out of conviction that Christians should not participate in activities like that.

They will not allow men and women to go swimming together. There is a de-emphasis on the ways of the world. And it will also be coupled with, "Don't watch television; spend your time reading the Scriptures." I've seen a lot of that in Christian churches that I call Christian brothers, but that's not my persuasion, you know.

JUDGE SEYRANIAN: *But is that a way of holding the people to the religion more than if that principle was not one of the teachings of the church or that religion? I mean do you think that the reason they do that is, in your opinion, to hold these people and get them more involved, or is it just the practice or principles they believe?*

DR. MALONY: I would hope that's the reason they do it, because, you see, there is a higher theological reason above that, that it is the job of the Christian to so live in this world that they glorify God and are prepared for heaven.

You have to remember that the "Local Church" is in a great body of churches throughout Christian history that would be called, for the judge's term, Separatists. They withdraw from the world, but they do it in a quite different way from the Amish or Mennonites. Remember, I think as far as I can tell, most of the "Local Church" people drive cars. I don't see the Spiritual Counterfeits Project going out after the Mennonites. God knows if they want to get somebody who really withdraws, take them on.

As far as I can tell, I've never seen any unusual dress in these people. In the survey that I took, one man said to me, "Yes, the brothers' house that I lived in didn't take a newspaper and didn't have a television, but I went out and bought mine every day because I wanted to read the news."

Sure, my answer originally was, I hope it does, because that is the theological bent for us to spend the time we have preparing ourselves for heaven. Now I said the secular person would say, "Oh, that's bad," because the secular, non-religious person would not have that motivation and would tend to believe that all religion was world-denying.

MR. MORGAN: *Maybe you better explain the expression "world-denying."*

DR. MALONY: That your job is to avoid the temptations of the world. And Saint Paul writes a lot about that. You know, that's not bad ground for theological thinking.

MR. MORGAN: *And are there certain denominations that are readily accepted in the Christian community that feel very strongly about this separating from or denying the world in that religious sense?*

DR. MALONY: Oh, yes.

MR. MORGAN: *Can you name some of them?*

DR. MALONY: Church of Christ, for example, many primitive Baptist groups, even some Southern Baptist groups, Mennonites, Amish, Apostolic Church of America, Brethren in Christ. Give me a list of denominations, and I would say that fully a third of the Christian denominations still feel that way.

In the sociology of religion, there has been the term "Sect church," and it is said that many of the denominations began as Separatists' movements, withdrawn from the world, world-denying, but became, over time—I don't mean this pejoratively—culturally accommodating, meaning they made their accommodation with the culture.

My own church is probably a better example than any of this. The United Methodists began in England in the 1700s, and I doubt if any historian of religion would back away from calling it a sect. It was a break-off from the Church of England. And the teachings of John Wesley were immensely Separatist.

There were weekly meetings where the chief question was, "What is the state of your soul; how much temptation have you undergone this week?" Most social analysts would now say it is very much a church that interacts with the world and does not consider itself Separatist. All of its members would have televisions.

MR. MORGAN: *Let me ask this question. Does the author try to create an image that these Christian beliefs that you have just discussed are some form of cult activity?*

DR. MALONY: Yes. I think that's definitely the emphasis, which makes the writer have a strange bedfellow, it seems to me. That's the same kind of comment that secular, non-religious social and behavioral scientists have made since the time of Sigmund Freud.

JUDGE SEYRANIAN: *Doctor, you might help me here. As I understand, the book doesn't use the word "cult." Is that correct?*

DR. MALONY: That may be correct. I think it uses the phrase "cult type." And in the appendix of this group, it quotes persons who have studied the cults, the Transcendental Meditationists, Moonies, and the like.

JUDGE SEYRANIAN: *Hari Krishnas?*

DR. MALONY: Hari Krishnas. And without any question, it says that the "Local Church" has these qualities. Now why else would they use those authorities who have studied cults? I mean the word "cult" is all over the final chapter or two.

JUDGE SEYRANIAN: *What you are saying is, the inferences are there even if they don't use the word per se "cult"?*

DR. MALONY: There is so much there that not only you but others I have had to talk to had to remind me that the church was not called a "cult." I was convinced after the first reading that they were called "cult." I had to go back. I don't think they ever used that word and probably that's by design. But after my first reading, there is no question in my mind as to what the import was.

JUDGE SEYRANIAN: *Maybe I'm way out in left field, but I'm trying to understand. This is a subject that is theological, and I'm trying to put the right emphasis where cults fit and where they don't fit. It is not the easiest thing in the world for me.*

If a religion holds its people in the sense by saying, we discourage TV watching, we discourage sports activities, which gives you more time to study this religion, to do the things that we believe in, the reading of the Bible and the understanding of these texts, and so forth. Okay, we say that that's the furtherance of that religion and that's the way that they practice their religion. That's okay.

Then we get on the other group, and let's take these other people on the other side, the "cults." They say, look, we hold these people, we hold them here so that they can spend more time with us and do things that we believe.

Where does the difference come in?

DR. MALONY: I don't think the difference is on that basis.

JUDGE SEYRANIAN: *Is the end result what they each believe in rather than how they do it?*

DR. MALONY: What they believe in is the distinction that the social scientists would make. That's the way I would define a cult, as on the basis of beliefs.

JUDGE SEYRANIAN: *What that religion or cult stands for, what its teachings and principles are. Is that what you are saying?*

DR. MALONY: I think that's primarily where I would draw the line.

JUDGE SEYRANIAN: *See, because we define cults by names of organizations, but I don't know, from a technical standpoint, exactly what these organizations really believe in.*

Like if we use the Moonies, we all heard that they use brainwashing and so forth. Well, that might be a method in which they hold their members.

DR. MALONY: Yes.

JUDGE SEYRANIAN: *What is it, in your opinion, that says they are not good, that's a cult, and that's bad?*

DR. MALONY: Let me back up a minute. As a social scientist, I use the term "cult" neutrally. I don't say good or bad. I use what I think is the dictionary and social-scientific understanding of the word "cult," which is, a cult is that kind of religious group which is not indigenous to your culture.

Now that makes the Christian faith a cult in the Roman world, and it was. Social historians say that's exactly true; the Christian faith was a cult in the Roman world up until the time of Constantine who, by fiat, made the whole Roman Empire Christian, and it is no longer a cult.

That's a very neutral definition. You have in America a plurality of religious groups so that who is a cult and who is not a cult, on that basis, is becoming much more difficult to say. What is indigenous American religion, particularly in California? Well, I think you do have to have some "standard orthodoxy." They call us a Christian nation, which is a very interesting description, because the United States became Christian sometime mid-century of the 1900s in terms of whether the majority of the people ascribe to "the Christian faith" over all denominations. We have been called a Christian nation largely because of the founding fathers' supposedly somewhat Unitarian points of view. We have been a pluralistic nation.

When you come to the people like the Moonies, I know that most Christians, and I would probably agree here, would call their theology heterodox, or completely outside the pale of the Christian faith, even though they would have some affinity with it. And from that point of view, let's say it is not indigenous to the United States, therefore, it's a "cult." But, I know when I use that word outside of scientific circles, that has a value judgment placed with it. That means "bad."

JUDGE SEYRANIAN: *That's right. The average person today who would read this book that we are talking about, if they got the connotation that it was a cult, would their feelings be it's bad, in your opinion?*

DR. MALONY: Bad and dangerous. Don't get involved.

JUDGE SEYRANIAN: *Okay. Now you have got to help me a little bit further.*

DR. MALONY: Okay.

JUDGE SEYRANIAN: *When we are talking about the common layman's understanding of a cult that's bad and dangerous, they associate it with certain organizations. We know Jim Jones, because he caused so many of those people to kill themselves. What is it, in your opinion, that is bad with respect to these cults?*

DR. MALONY: I'm formulating this sort of right now. I would think two things. One is a centralized authority. The second is manipulating social processes for devious ends.

JUDGE SEYRANIAN: *Okay.*

DR. MALONY: In that case, you have got to prove there is a charismatic figure who has that kind of authority and uses it in a way that manipulates social influence for devious ends, for ends that are not fully apparent.

JUDGE SEYRANIAN: *And would those ends be good ends or evil ends?*

DR. MALONY: Well, the implication of a cult is that they are devious ends. The presumption is made that the cult leader primarily wants control over the persons, though they may use an ideology which says, I'm telling you about the divine light, or I'm telling you about the Christian faith, that the real motivation is social or personal, individual control.

JUDGE SEYRANIAN: *That helps me a great deal, what you just said then. Some of this stuff I understand, but I think we are getting at the heart of it because we are doing a lot of talking about cults but not really trying to understand it. You are helping me now to understand it.*

DR. MALONY: Okay.

MR. MORGAN: *Let me pursue that a little further, Doctor. Is it your opinion that Exhibit 1 is conveying to the readers that in this case Witness Lee is that charismatic leader who is engaging in deceit and manipulating the minds of the people in the church for some devious purposes and to gain control of them?*

DR. MALONY: Yes. The book is saying Witness Lee knows all there is to know about social influence processes and has intentionally decided to use them on individuals and groups under pretense of one thing, and what Witness Lee really wants, his primary goal, is to have control of people's lives.

MR. MORGAN: *And based upon your study and investigation, is that totally false?*

DR. MALONY: I think it's invalid. Totally false.

MR. MORGAN: *Thank you. Now let's go to the test that you took. Let me mark this as Exhibit 24.*

(Questions and summary of responses in survey by Dr. Malony marked for identification as Exhibit 24.)

Let me show you what has been marked as Exhibit 24. And first I will ask you if you can identify what that is?

DR. MALONY: Yes. Exhibit 24 is a four-page document; the first page is a list of twenty questions which I used in a survey for five groups, and pages two, three, and four are summary tables of the responses to those questions.

MR. MORGAN: *Okay. I'll offer that into evidence.*

JUDGE SEYRANIAN: *It may be admitted in evidence.*

QUESTIONS USED IN TELEPHONE INTERVIEW

In your experience at the church:

1. Were you told who to marry?
2. Were you told where to live?
3. Did the leaders control your finances?
4. Did the leaders tell you where to work?
5. Was the reading of newspapers or looking at TV or listening to the radio discouraged?
6. Were you told when or where to go to school?
7. Were you ever counseled by church leaders about your behavior?
8. Were you pressured to take the advice of church leaders?
9. Were you ever chastised publicly by church leaders?
10. Were you ever encouraged to behave unethically by church leaders? to lie? to deceive?
11. Was the church misrepresented to you? Did you know and understand what you were getting into?
12. As a result of church worship, did you ever go into a trance? Did you feel spacy? Confused? Out of control? Hypnotized?
13. As a result of church worship, did you ever feel like

you had to obey the leaders without thinking things through on your own?
14. Do you study the Bible on your own? What Bible helps do you use in your study?
15. Have you ever felt brainwashed? Coerced?
16. What role does Witness Lee (John Wesley) play in your faith?
17. Is the Local Church the only church?
18. How long have you been (were you) a member of the Local Church?
19. When and how did you become a Christian?
20. Who is Jesus Christ?

MR. MORGAN: *Now let's start out this way. First, will you tell the court the rationale behind going forward with this type of an examination?*

DR. MALONY: Yes. In my reading of the documents used in the accusations against the "Local Church," I was impressed with what I felt to be an inadequate and confusing methodology on the part of the social and behavioral scientist used by the accusers. I had some immediate questions, such as: Why did they not interview or talk to present members? Also another question: Why did they not compare their impressions with other Christian groups to see if some of the same predominant practices were going on there? And why did they not interview some other ex-members to see if the reports that they were getting were typical? They seemed to presume some interesting over-generalizations.

MR. MORGAN: *All right. Now can you tell the court, then, again in just general terms, what you did by way of the examination, then we'll get to the specifics. Precisely what did you do in this regard?*

DR. MALONY: I asked the "Local Church" to provide me with the membership list of two of their churches, from which I selected, using a table of random numbers, a representative sample in each church of fifteen members from each church, present members.

MR. MORGAN: *You say by a random sample?*

DR. MALONY: Yes.

MR. MORGAN: *Can you describe to the court how you go about that?*
DR. MALONY: Well, random sample basically means a non-systematic sample. Like if you took every fourth name, that's a system. A random sample takes a table which scrambles numbers in a way that investigators know how to use and generate out what looks like a hodgepodge of names, the first one, the twentieth one.
MR. MORGAN: *What is the purpose in doing it that way?*
DR. MALONY: Well, the assumptions underlying statistical tests, to know whether the differences that you get could have occurred by chance or not, always presume that you have taken a random sample as opposed to a systematic sample. So it's one of the presumptions of statistical tests, a random sample.

For example, you can make fairly accurate generalizations, it has been proven, on the basis of very small random samples. Several years ago, we did a one-percent random sample of research, and it gave us 750 people out of 50,000, I can't remember the exact number, and we were able to print that in a professional journal as characterizing the whole group. That's what you do; you make inferences in your sample to what is true in the whole group.

I feel very confident that the samples I took from present members are a worthy and accurate reflection of what goes on in present members in these two churches.
MR. MORGAN: *That was one category. What was another category?*
DR. MALONY: I went to Methodist churches in the same community, one in Fullerton. The Methodist pastor cooperated with me in Anaheim because I knew him. He gave me a selective sample from his church, meaning his is not a random sample, so I have less confidence in that.

I went to the pastor in Fullerton who didn't know me; he promised to give me a list. He didn't. I went to a church in Sierra Madre. I picked out seven in Anaheim and seven in Sierra Madre. These are both selected samples.
MR. MORGAN: *So now on one side, you have the present members of the "Local Church"; you have reports.*

DR. MALONY: Present members of the Methodist Church, which I would consider a traditional, mainline church.

MR. MORGAN: *What else did you do?*

DR. MALONY: I asked the "Local Church" to provide me with a list of ex-members, and they did so. Again, they gave me a list of about fifteen or sixteen. I was able to make contact with thirteen, a number living in distant cities. They were very cooperative. I think you would have to say, this, too, is not a random sample. I did not have a list of all the ex-members of all the churches of America from which to take a random sample. I asked the "Local Church" to simply give me as many as they could find.

MR. MORGAN: *Did you feel that what you were given was sufficient to assist you in performing this test?*

DR. MALONY: Yes. I would want you to call it action research. It's not fully controlled. I would say that this selected sample of ex-members is about as representative as any other selected sample.

In other words, we have got a group over here that's mad at the church, and here is a group that has left, and we are going to ask them questions. I don't know whether one is more representative than the other for sure, but I certainly have some faith in this.

MR. MORGAN: *Was there in addition a fourth category that you used; did you get ex-members from any other church?*

DR. MALONY: No.

MR. MORGAN: *Okay.*

DR. MALONY: I know a bunch of ex-members from other churches, and seemingly I've heard some of the same gripes. I have seen Baptist churches split where SCP surely would not want to get a hold of them. They are saying some of the same things about the leaders.

MR. MORGAN: *Then you formulated some questions to ask to these groups.*

DR. MALONY: Yes.

MR. MORGAN: *And did each of these questions relate to some charge in the book?*

DR. MALONY: Indeed. That's where I got the questions.

MR. MORGAN: *Okay. And then how did you perform the examination?*
DR. MALONY: By telephone. All the interviews were performed by telephone.
MR. MORGAN: *And then did you tabulate all of those results?*
DR. MALONY: I did.
MR. MORGAN: *All right. Now let's start with the first question on Exhibit 24, and it says, "Were you told who to marry?"*
DR. MALONY: Yes.
MR. MORGAN: *To assist the court in that regard, Your Honor, if you will go to a portion from the Duddy manuscript:*

> The regulation of intimacy reached its fullest expression in a northwestern U.S. Local Church where marriages were arranged by elders and their wives between people who were only casually acquainted with one another. Couples were paired according to the elders' consentient belief that God was leading them to arrange marriages among the good brothers and sisters. In one month alone, this matchmaking yielded more than a baker's dozen of marriages under the guidance of the yenta-like elders' wives.
>
> The regulation of intimacy by Local Church authorities serves a dual purpose. First, the laity's submission to church leaders insures the individual's burial. Relinquishing all personal responsibility and authority for their lives (e.g., choice of a marriage partner) signals total vulnerability among church members.

And I might add to the court that we are going to introduce evidence that the "baker's dozen of marriages" never took place. But that will come from another witness. Was that basically what this question was relating to?
DR. MALONY: Yes.
MR. MORGAN: *Will you tell the court your findings in that regard?*
DR. MALONY: No one of the present members, no one of the ex-members, and no Methodist reported their marriages were arranged.
MR. MORGAN: *Okay. Let's go to number two: "Were you told where to live?"*

DR. MALONY: It had to do with living within three miles of the church, moving close enough.

MR. MORGAN: That's right. There is something in that vein. Would you tell the court what your results were in that regard?

DR. MALONY: No one of the present members, no one of the ex-members, and no Methodists were told where to live.

MR. MORGAN: Fine. Let's go to number three: "Did the leaders control your finances?"

DR. MALONY: Once again, no one of the present members, no ex-members, and no Methodists said that their finances were controlled.

MR. MORGAN: Okay. Number four: "Did the leaders tell you where to work?"

DR. MALONY: No one of the present members, no one of the ex-members, no Methodists were told where to work.

MR. MORGAN: Let's go to number five: "Was the reading of newspapers or looking at TV or listening to the radio discouraged?"

DR. MALONY: Three of the present members, that's three out of thirty, three of the ex-members, one of the Methodists were discouraged.

MR. MORGAN: So we have three out of thirty of present members. Three out of thirteen of the ex-members. And then one out of fourteen Methodists. Okay.

DR. MALONY: Now I would like to say to the court that the inferential statistical test that would be performed on data such as this to ask whether one group differed from another would be a Chi Square analysis. A Chi Square analysis of this data said these results were chance variations, not due to something other than chance. That's the way you reason.

MR. MORGAN: Okay. Can you sort of translate that for us? What does that mean, then, to you in making this test?

DR. MALONY: That means if I had taken thirty other present members, thirteen other ex-members, fourteen other Methodists, I might have gotten different results, which would, over the replication of this test a hundred times, vary just by chance in terms of which group had the highest and which group had the lowest. Does that make sense? Let me put it this way. In other words, if you got ten of the present members and seven of the ex-members, and none of the Methodists, I feel confident that Chi Square analysis would tell you something other than chance is occurring.

MR. MORGAN: *So you are saying that if you got that kind of a report, that would indicate to you that it was fairly probable that was discouraged?*

DR. MALONY: That was discouraged.

MR. MORGAN: *All right.*

JUDGE SEYRANIAN: *Let me see if I understand that. Are you saying, then, from the number that you got, if you were to try to put the position of the "Local Church" with respect to this question, would you say that based on these answers, the "Local Church" does or does not discourage reading newspapers?*

DR. MALONY: Here is the sort of statement we make. There is no statistical evidence that the "Local Church" discourages looking at television or reading newspapers or listening to the radio any more than do the Methodists. But let me hasten to add, that surprises me, because the "Local Church" is as I said a while ago, in general terms, a Separatist church, and one would expect them to discourage looking at television.

If this was a Southern Baptist sample, I have a feeling that the leaders of the Southern Baptist Church would say, "I'm very sorry that doesn't show that our church discourages it more than the Methodists." Do you understand what I am saying? If I were a "Local Church" member, I would say, "Oh, that's discouraging." I'm just being facetious.

MR. MORGAN: *Let me ask you this. In asking the questions, did anyone indicate to you that the "Local Church" forbade the watching of movies or television or reading the papers?*

DR. MALONY: No. Now that's an interesting thing. In no case did they forbid. For some of the qualifications in these answers, they said, "Well, I lived in a brother's house where the mother and father did not take a newspaper or watch television, but nobody ever told me not to. It was more peer pressure, what everybody else was doing, than it was the leaders."

Now they said, "The leaders did encourage us to spend what spare time we had serving the Lord. At lunch time, if you have got a few minutes, read the Bible or try to attend all the meetings of the church." But, you know, I again would hasten to add, we are making qualitative judgments here. In church life, in pastoral life, there is a lot of talk about how much time you are spending at the church as opposed to how much time you are spending with your family. It's not only the "Local Church" that requires people to be there every night.

MR. MORGAN: *Okay. I might point out to the court, there is the statement in the Duddy manuscript and in the German edition, and it reads:*

> Local Church policy expands the New Testament mandate to shed immorality to include forbidding members to watch television, read newspapers, or go to movie theaters.

That was carried over into Die Sonderlehre. *But when it got to the one published by Inter-Varsity Press, it comes out more of discouraging than prohibiting. And so that was what we worked at on that one.*

DR. MALONY: By the way, many of us grew up in churches in the South, where the old adage, "I don't smoke, I don't chew, and I don't go with the girls that do," was very pervasive. You definitely didn't go to movies; you didn't buy phonograph records; you didn't listen to the radio. All those were worldly activities. It's not new with the "Local Church."

MR. MORGAN: *Put in another context, there is nothing that makes it a cult if a minister or a leader encourages the people not to watch television and not to go to the movies and not to read newspapers, but spend that time learning the Lord and being a part of the Lord's work?*

DR. MALONY: Not unless you want to call a lot of conservative churches cults.

MR. MORGAN: *Okay. Fine. Let's go on to number six: "Were you told when and where to go to school?"*

DR. MALONY: None of the present members, none of the

ex-members, and no Methodists were told where to go to school or when to go to school.

MR. MORGAN: *Number seven: "Were you ever counseled by church leaders about your behavior?"*

DR. MALONY: One of the present members, one of the ex-members, none of the Methodists.

MR. MORGAN: *What, if anything, does that indicate to you?*

DR. MALONY: It may indicate that the pastors of the Methodist Church weren't exercising good pastoral behavior. I'm being facetious there. I would hope that church leaders would counsel church members about their behavior. This is another one of those things where I think the implication of the book is that people were called to elders' meetings and chastised and humiliated in the same way that number nine talks about chastising publicly. I think that is the import. That's the way I asked the question.

MR. MORGAN: Okay. *What is your conclusion?*

DR. MALONY: My conclusion is that there are no differences across the group.

JUDGE SEYRANIAN: *Is this another question where you feel the "Local Church" leaders would hope there were more yeses?*

DR. MALONY: Yes. And I believe the Methodist leaders would have hoped there were more yeses. I believe the Catholic priest would have hoped there were more yeses.

MR. MORGAN: *Number eight: "Were you pressured to take the advice of church leaders?"*

DR. MALONY: None of the present members, two out of thirteen of the ex-members, and none of the Methodists reported being pressured.

MR. MORGAN: *Again, what does that indicate to you?*

DR. MALONY: I think statistical tests on this would say no difference between the groups. Though two of the ex-members did report that they felt at some time or another pressured. Two out of thirteen. Probably chance variation.

MR. MORGAN: *Again, what would that indicate to you as to what was in fact the practice in the church?*

DR. MALONY: Well, as one person said to me, "I was counseled and then told to pray about it and seek the Lord's will."

MR. MORGAN: *And does this response give you any indication that the church members are told that they must follow the elders or leaders?*
DR. MALONY: Absolutely no. I think that would be an invalid presumption.
MR. MORGAN: *Number nine: "Were you ever chastised publicly by church leaders?"*
DR. MALONY: None of the present members, none of the ex-members, and none of the Methodists were chastised publicly.
MR. MORGAN: *Number ten: "Were you ever encouraged to behave unethically by church leaders? to lie? to deceive?"*
DR. MALONY: None of the present members, none of the ex-members, and none of the Methodists reported such.
MR. MORGAN: *And this, of course, goes to the teaching that he is advocating immorality?*
DR. MALONY: I got some strong reactions counter to this, saying quite the reverse. "We were always encouraged to behave ethically."
MR. MORGAN: *And would that be also from the ex-members?*
DR. MALONY: Yes. The fact is that I remember that strongest from one of the ex-members.
MR. MORGAN: *Number eleven: "Was the church misrepresented to you? Did you know and understand what you were getting into?"*
DR. MALONY: This question, as you can realize, was a no-yes question.
MR. MORGAN: *All right.*
DR. MALONY: "'Was the church misrepresented?" None of the present members, none of the ex-members, and none of the Methodists reported the church being misrepresented to them. That goes to the seduction issue, deviant motive, thought you were getting one thing and got another.
MR. MORGAN: *That's the "seduction syndrome" Mr. Duddy created?*
DR. MALONY: Yes.
MR. MORGAN: *And the answers there show it was totally false?*
DR. MALONY: Yes.
MR. MORGAN: *How about the second phase of the question?*

DR. MALONY: It reversed. All of the present members, all of the ex-members, and all of the Methodists reported they knew what they were getting into.

MR. MORGAN: *Was that of some significance to you?*

DR. MALONY: That was two sides of the same question.

MR. MORGAN: *Fine. Let's go to number twelve: "As a result of church worship, did you ever go into a trance? Did you feel spacy? Confused? Out of control? Hypnotized?" Now first, can you explain to His Honor why this question is being asked?*

DR. MALONY: Well, the book talked about altered states of consciousness, as if the church meetings were basically of two or three types. One is the training session led by Witness Lee that will begin or end with a testing where people stand up and he asks them questions or they volunteer. Another is a regular Sunday morning led by the elders. The third would be the pray-reading sessions which often occur midweek or on Saturday; I'm unclear, and they asked me what did I mean, and I mentioned all three of those.

MR. MORGAN: *Why are you asking this question?*

DR. MALONY: Because the inference, if not the outright accusation, was that these events caused persons to lose mental control, lose rationality, become hyper-sensuous and emotional, even go into an altered state of consciousness, at which time, according to this interpretation of the literature, they become very susceptible to leader influence, leader commands, as in a hypnotic state.

MR. MORGAN: *And again, is this sort of the popular conception of a cult leader?*

DR. MALONY: Of a cult leader or a cult situation. Yes.

MR. MORGAN: *Would you tell the court your findings in that regard?*

DR. MALONY: One out of thirty present members, one out of thirteen ex-members, and none of the Methodists reported that experience.

MR. MORGAN: *What did that indicate to you?*

DR. MALONY: Those are chance variations. There are no differences between groups.

MR. MORGAN: *Okay. Did you personally participate?*
DR. MALONY: Yes. In all three of those.
MR. MORGAN: *Let's take the pray-reading. Was there anything in that experience that in any way could cause you to become in an altered state of consciousness where somebody could then get hold of your mind?*
DR. MALONY: I certainly did not feel so, and I went incognito. I went as a participant/observer and, in fact, entered into the worship experience, which is an experience of either taking the Bible at a certain passage or taking printed verses from the Bible and reading them through together in a way that does not differ radically from what my church does on Sunday morning in what is called responsive reading. When I say radically, it was different because after the verse is read through completely, everybody reading it, then the practice is to go back to the first part of the verse and read it phrase by phrase and make comments after each phrase is read.

One person might say, "I will lift up mine eyes unto the hills from whence cometh my help," Psalm 121. Everybody would read that. Then somebody would start it, very spontaneous leadership, "I will lift up mine eyes. Praise the Lord! Thank goodness for ability to lift up mine eyes! I WILL lift up mine eyes. I will LIFT up mine eyes." There is a fair amount of Amening and "Thank you, Jesus" that goes on with that, though I must say that I was expecting a real blowout experience. And my thought was, after I left, that whoever wrote this book sure hadn't been around. You know, I've been in many revival and testimony periods that were much more persuasive and moving than that, as far as going into whatever might be called an altered state of consciousness.

JUDGE SEYRANIAN: *What you are making reference to is what they call their pray-reading?*
DR. MALONY: Yes. It's reading of the Scripture, very focused on the Scriptures.
JUDGE SEYRANIAN: *There are other churches that perform similar things where everybody gets somewhat emotional in the sense that you are getting on a high?*

DR. MALONY: A high, that's right.

JUDGE SEYRANIAN: *And as a psychologist, what is the reason for doing this? Is there a reason why this is done?*

DR. MALONY: In the "Local Church" or wherever?

JUDGE SEYRANIAN: *I think there is a similar practice done in some other churches.*

DR. MALONY: Oh, I also think so.

JUDGE SEYRANIAN: *What is the reason? Is there some reason why you think this is done?*

DR. MALONY: Well, you have to realize that not only throughout Christian history but in the psychology of religion, there is this whole thing; religion is what you believe and what you experience. Christian history is replete with movements which start out as experience movements and then become fairly ritualistic and dogmatic. And then there will be another group that critiques them, and they rise up, and they have experiences, and they go over history.

Both of those facets, Christian experience and Christian belief, have been important facts of Christian experience down through the centuries. So what this is intended to do is deepen one's Christian experience.

I know that the "Local Church" has a theology behind that that has to do with imbibing the word, making the word come to life, which, you know, I hadn't heard about before, but I found a fairly refreshing counterpart to this kind of word study which takes the Hebrew or Greek and, God knows, goes back and tries to repeat that.

JUDGE SEYRANIAN: *I'm asking you as a psychologist, now, as a man who has studied psychology for many, many years, this type of reading of a passage and spontaneous explanation and so forth, what does it do to a person? How does it put them in a state of mind? What does it do to their state of mind?*

DR. MALONY: Oh, I think it expands it. I love the words "mind expansion."

JUDGE SEYRANIAN: *What do you mean by "mind expansion"?*

DR. MALONY: Well, it takes them, so to speak, out of

any presumption that life is really lived entirely in the frontal lobe of the brain.

JUDGE SEYRANIAN: *Does it take them out of the world of reality for that moment?*

DR. MALONY: Well, another way of saying it, it might put them into the real reality. You know, one of our fairly contemporary theoreticians, Fritz Pearls, the Gestalt psychologist, says that the primary way to do therapy is to get out of your mind and come to your senses.

And we talk in our therapy about getting in touch with all of you. And the Hebrew understanding of the human being is a mind-body-soul complex.

It seems to me that this book, and much of contemporary social science, really has bought into a twentieth century view of what reality is all about, a scientific point of view which is hyper-rational; it has no experiential dimension. Anybody who has been to Catholic mass knows that the Catholic Church never bought into that.

MR. MORGAN: *Doctor, let's go back to the pray-reading for a moment. The purpose of the pray-reading, can you indicate this is some form of a devotional function of the church or of this church?*

DR. MALONY: It is. I would think of it as worship, very much similar to the practices of the church throughout the years, of supposedly "deepening the Christian life."

MR. MORGAN: *Can you give us some analogies of other churches? Let's take the Catholic Church; is there something that might be considered comparable?*

DR. MALONY: Well, I was thinking of the saying of the rosary, the mass itself, certainly if you took the rule of Saint Benedict.

MR. MORGAN: *Which I don't know. You have got to tell me that.*

DR. MALONY: Well, like many monastic orders, they are built on a rule or a way of life defined by a given charismatic figure like a saint, which would order the days. Then, for example, one of the practices in the Benedictine rule would be to take a passage of Scripture, meditate on it, and say it over and over again to yourself, and come back to your spiritual confessor or adviser. Or it may be more like the Ignatian Rule.

MR. MORGAN: *Or the Eastern Orthodox, the Jesus Prayer could be comparable?*

DR. MALONY: Yes.

MR. MORGAN: *One of the concepts of the book is that this is a form of hypnotism. Since you participated in it, will you give the court your observations as to whether this practice could in any way be a form of hypnotism?*

DR. MALONY: Well, I don't think so, in terms of what we understand to be hypnotism, so to speak, in the trade or where the term is technically used. Though hypnotism has pretty much of a long history, it's a contemporary term that applies to an old process, putting people in a state in which they can, so to speak, get in touch with their unconscious or either follow the directions of a leader.

But, I would hasten to add, our understanding of hypnotism as a process is, a person will never submit to following a leader's commands unless they inwardly and deeply want to do what the leader is telling them to do.

MR. MORGAN: *Let me ask you this. On the pray-reading that you participated in, first, was there some leader that was directing how they were doing this thing?*

DR. MALONY: If there was, I couldn't find who that was. And I was there from the beginning. I felt the person who began it was going to be a leader, but that leadership shifted all around, and another person closed the event that day.

MR. MORGAN: *And when the event was closed, was there then some intent to instill in the minds of the people some particular principle at that moment?*

DR. MALONY: No sir, as far as I could tell. It was, "Time's up, let's have a cup of coffee."

MR. MORGAN: *Again going back, were you hypnotized in any way by going through this process?*

DR. MALONY: No. I found it to be an important experience, one I will remember, certainly not negative.

MR. MORGAN: *In what respect?*

DR. MALONY: I was impressed with the sharing, which was a lovely experience. It was not negative.

MR. MORGAN: *When you use the term "sharing," what do you mean?*

DR. MALONY: As the verses were being read through, phrase by phrase, one person might say, "I had the Lord close to me yesterday when I was working, and my boss told me to do something I didn't want to do, but I just prayed to the Lord to be with me, and I got through the day." And the rest of the people would say, "Amen." It was primarily sharing like that.

MR. MORGAN: *Did it indicate to you the people were in fact using their minds?*

DR. MALONY: Certainly. They were certainly not out of their minds. They were relating it to their daily experience. The whole event was focused on a set of written Scriptures, quite unlike, say, a more charismatic worship experience which is somewhat typical of other places. I would hasten to add, this didn't feel like a non-cognitive experience.

MR. MORGAN: *Let's talk about the mantra. Are you familiar with a mantra?*

DR. MALONY: Yes.

MR. MORGAN: *Was this a mantra where you repeat things you don't know?*

DR. MALONY: Or repeat them over and over. In the appendix of this book it compares this to a mantra. Then it goes ahead to explain how a mantra is to be used in both Transcendental Meditation and the Hare Krishna movement. In those cases, a mantra is supposed to be repeated for hours at a time. This whole experience lasted an hour and a half, and we went over four pages of Scripture. So there is no one phrase being repeated in any repetitive way by any means. I've talked to some other folks, and I gather I was in on a very typical experience.

MR. MORGAN: Okay. Let's go to the next question, number thirteen: "As a result of church worship, did you ever feel like you had to obey the leaders without thinking things through on your own?"

DR. MALONY: None of the present members, two of the thirteen ex-members, and none of the Methodists felt that way.

MR. MORGAN: *And what did those figures, indicate to you?*

DR. MALONY: Chance variation, no difference between groups. I think that particular question was directed toward the presumption that under a trance state, as in question twelve, or under a hypnotic state, a person might be told something to do and do it kind of as an automaton or zombie, without thinking it through. The book also presumes that what the persons are told to do will be evil.

MR. MORGAN: *The two that said "Yes" to that, did they give any comments?*

DR. MALONY: They qualified it and said that they took it more to be the group exhilaration, the pressure of the group experience.

MR. MORGAN: *Number fourteen: "Do you study the Bible on your own? What Bible helps do you use in your study?" First, can you tell the court why this question was asked?*

DR. MALONY: It had to do with the accusations that the people were told entirely how to study the Bible and that they were always under control when they did study it, as if there were some distortion going on.

MR. MORGAN: *In other words, that the leaders are telling the people this is what you will read and this is all you will read and this is what you must interpret and, in effect, you can't do your own thinking?*

DR. MALONY: Yes, and of course, the implication is that all they had were the writings of Witness Lee to study.

MR. MORGAN: *Right.*

DR. MALONY: I did not report the figures here because everybody said they studied the Bible on their own. And the variety of helps that they said they used were just all over the map from one person saying, "Well, I had a concordance," or "I used the writings of Darby," or "I went to see the writings of the Brethren," or "I just read it on my own."

I think, by the way, that if I were Witness Lee, I would be a little embarrassed how few times they mentioned they studied my books or used them when they did self-study. It certainly was not an imperialistic "This is the only thing we read," you see.

MR. MORGAN: *And what does that indicate to you?*

DR. MALONY: It indicated that the accusation that their minds were being controlled by input from as far as what they were using to study the Bible was a false accusation.

MR. MORGAN: *Let me go on to the next one, number fifteen: "Have you ever felt brainwashed? Coerced?"*

DR. MALONY: None of the present members, one out of thirteen of the ex-members, and none of the Methodists felt that way. And I concluded chance variation. Questions fifteen, thirteen, and twelve are related, you see.

MR. MORGAN: *In the course of that, did you come across a comment by any ex-member about the conduct of another ex-member?*

DR. MALONY: Yes.

MR. MORGAN: *Okay. And what was that in response to?*

DR. MALONY: Well, it was an interesting comment, and I can't remember whether it was the one that reported they felt brainwashed or not, but there was one ex-member who said, "Yes, I felt it, definitely, from one leader who has now left the church and whose behavior was not characteristic of the leaders of the church."

MR. MORGAN: *Okay.*

DR. MALONY: You want me to name the leader?

MR. MORGAN: *Sure. Did the person name the leader?*

DR. MALONY: Yes. A person named Rapoport.

MR. MORGAN: *Let's now go to number sixteen: "What role does Witness Lee (John Wesley) play in your faith?" Now can you explain the question first?*

DR. MALONY: The question had to do with the accusation of Witness Lee exercising, as the text said, almost papal authority, and the inference being that he was somehow even quasi-divine, somehow having a special role. And I asked the Methodists, their leader would be John Wesley, the founder of the church in the 1700s, and Witness Lee would be the parallel to today.

MR. MORGAN: *What results did you get?*

DR. MALONY: And again, these are all anecdotal, so I couldn't summarize them. Witness Lee was pictured as an elder brother, a teacher, a respected leader. Each of them said that Witness Lee was important to them. I was embarrassed; many of the Methodists didn't remember who John Wesley was. Then I prefaced that question with a subsequent question: "Is Witness Lee Divine?" And there was no uniformity, "Of course not," that sort of answer.

MR. MORGAN: *When you use the word "Divine," that has a special significance?*

DR. MALONY: Yes.

MR. MORGAN: *What does it mean?*

DR. MALONY: Is he somehow a God? Does he have a special place over and above being simply a leader? And there was denial throughout.

MR. MORGAN: *And that's both ex-members as well as present members?*

DR. MALONY: Across the board. No difference there.

MR. MORGAN: *So, basically, he was looked upon as either an elder person—*

DR. MALONY: An elder brother, a person who teaches us the Scripture, a leader, answers I think that might be given to any important leader in a group. No difference.

MR. MORGAN: *Okay. Fine. Let's go to number seventeen: "Is the 'Local Church,' the only church?" What is the significance of that question?*

DR. MALONY: Well, to some extent, you have to remember that my wording of these questions reflects some misunderstanding of "Local Church" theology. I don't think they would ask that question in quite the same way. I don't think the "Local Church" would call any people members.

MR. MORGAN: *That's right.*

DR. MALONY: So I'm a little in error there. But what I was trying to get at was the exclusiveness that the accusations made, that people are told, "If you leave this, you are going to hell. If you don't come into it, you will never be saved."

MR. MORGAN: *"Your only chance is to be in this church." Is that basically the thrust?*

DR. MALONY: That's right. So I went ahead and prefaced this with everyone and said, "Are there other Christians outside the Local Church?" And this is a kind of no-yes question; no, the "Local Church" is not the only church.

All of the present members said no; all of the ex-members

said no; and all the Methodists said no. Then they answered yes to the other question: "Are there Christians outside the 'Local Church'"? Are there Christians outside the Methodist Church?" And they all said yes.

MR. MORGAN: *What does that signify to you?*

DR. MALONY: It signifies to me that they are not as Separatist as I thought they were. In other words, being the only church is something different groups have asserted down through the years. And I presumed that we would get the opposite here.

MR. MORGAN: *You thought that the members would say, "Yes, we are the only ones," but they said, "No"?*

DR. MALONY: Yes. They surprised me.

JUDGE SEYRANIAN: *Excuse me. Did you phrase the question at all, "Do you agree that the "Local Church" should be the only church"?*

DR. MALONY: No, I did not.

JUDGE SEYRANIAN: *That isn't part of this question, is it?*

DR. MALONY: No. But I understand the import of what you are saying. And as I understand, better now, the "Local Church" theology, it would be that denominational separatism, separating ourselves into denominations, is not the will of God, that we are to come together as Christians.

JUDGE SEYRANIAN: *You mean one church?*

DR. MALONY: One church in each local community. You have to remember, the Disciples of Christ in the nineteenth century were based on the same assumption. So this is not unique.

JUDGE SEYRANIAN: *I just wanted to know if that was part of the question.*

DR. MALONY: No, I did not ask that question.

MR. MORGAN: *Now, eighteen: "How long have you been or were you a member of the 'Local Church'?" What sort of response did you get there?*

DR. MALONY: What I have summarized is the average and then the range. There are significant differences here. I'm not sure what to make of it, but present members have been members of the "Local Church" an average of over 12.9 years, ranging from one to twenty-seven years—

somebody just come in, somebody who's been there twenty-seven years.

The ex-members were members or attended an average of 8.2 years with a range of two to sixteen years. And the Methodists have been members of the Methodist church thiry-one years on the average with a range between four and seventy years. So we must have gotten one of the older members there.

MR. MORGAN: *Okay. Now, number nineteen: "When and how did you become a Christian?" What is the significance of that question?*

DR. MALONY: I was interested in knowing whether all their Christian experience had occurred in the "Local Church." I didn't summarize it. This was anecdotal. The vast majority were Christians before they came into the "Local Church."

MR. MORGAN: *What is the significance of that, at least in your local study?*

DR. MALONY: From my study, it would be that this is not the only experience. It has not been so narrowly defined for them that they are limited in this point of view. Now to be sure, I would assume that most of those who came from other churches did so out of conviction that this was a better way, you know.

MR. MORGAN: *Right. And number twenty: "Who is Jesus Christ?"*

DR. MALONY: Yes.

MR. MORGAN: *Again, why was that question posed?*

DR. MALONY: I asked that to see if I could, in my kind of theological naiveté, get at the accusation that somehow the "Local Church" misconstrued the Trinity in some way. Modalism, I think, is the word they use, but I wouldn't want to be pressed exactly what that means. But I do feel that the answers I got were just plain orthodox answers, "Jesus is the Son of God," "Jesus is our Savior," "Jesus saves us from sin."

MR. MORGAN: *In other words, you didn't hear any responses that were different than you would expect to hear in any other Christian organization. Is that what you are saying?*

Dr. Malony: That is right. I heard one or two super liberal responses in the Methodist Church that I was ashamed of.

Judge Seyranian: *I have a question about this survey, and I want you to help me. I understand that when you take, for example, a lie detector test, before they give the person the lie detector test, they take a sample of something that is known to test what is going to happen on the machine.*

Dr. Malony: Yes.

Judge Seyranian: *They look, for example, at a brown wall and say, "Tell me if that color is white." The person says, "White," and he knows it is brown, and the machine starts jumping, and they know they have got a good test sample. When this person says a dishonest example, it is going to register on the machine.*

Dr. Malony: That's right.

Judge Seyranian: *What is bothering me here, if we determine with respect to questions five and seven that the "Local Church" does discourage reading of newspapers and looking at TV and listening to the radio, and we also find out that the "Local Church" does counsel their people with respect to their behavior, and yet these people all say "No," doesn't that affect the effectiveness of the survey as to how valid it is?*

If we have a couple of knowns in here and we have not really got the kind of answers that you would have liked to have had—

Mr. Morgan: *You are assuming that we have knowns.*

Judge Seyranian: *I'm saying, assuming that is the teaching of the church. We haven't gone into that specifically.*

Mr. Morgan: *That's right.*

Judge Seyranian: *If that were. Maybe we will determine that it does not turn out to be. Is there going to be testimony, Mr. Morgan, that reading newspapers, looking at TV, and listening to the radio are not discouraged?*

Mr. Morgan: *Is not discouraged. That's right. So I don't mislead the court, the teaching will be that you should spend as much time as you can with the Bible and with Christ. But there is no dogma set out that it's not good, you're not going to get to heaven, or anything like that.*

JUDGE SEYRANIAN: *The question doesn't say that. The question is: "Is reading of newspapers or looking at TV or listening to the radio discouraged?" Does the church discourage that or not?*

MR. MORGAN: *I believe the testimony will be that it does not. It doesn't encourage it, though.*

JUDGE SEYRANIAN: *I'm missing you. The question is, do they discourage? Does the church discourage reading of newspapers or looking at TV and listening to the radio?*

MR. MORGAN: *I believe the answer is "No," Your Honor.*

JUDGE SEYRANIAN: *They do not. All right. Their answers would be that.*

MR. MORGAN: *And I think the test shows that the people don't see it as being any discouraging. That's why I was a little concerned about the question, because I think that was the charge made in the book. The book said "forbidden." It didn't say "discouraged."*

JUDGE SEYRANIAN: *Yes, they go further.*

MR. MORGAN: *They say "forbidden," which is totally false. There is no discouraging, but certainly there is the encouraging of spending more time with the Bible. But that, I don't think, equates into discouraging the reading of the newspaper and the like. I should also add this, that there clearly is discouraging of watching things that are immoral.*

JUDGE SEYRANIAN: *Okay. I can understand that. The Catholic Church couldn't pass that test.*

MR. MORGAN: *That's right. I think any church would be the same.*

JUDGE SEYRANIAN: *Okay. I thought in some of the witnesses we had that they made an inference that was discouraged. Maybe I'm wrong. When we get the actual people from the church on the stand, we will be able to determine. If this was discouraged and the people said "No" when it should have been "Yes," I would have questions about the validity of this survey.*

DR. MALONY: Or I might have questions about whether they were listening. As you were talking, I had an interesting thought: The church teaches a lot of things people don't hear or the church would desire them to do a lot of things they don't do.

JUDGE SEYRANIAN: *Does the church counsel them with respect to their behavior?*

DR. MALONY: You also have to remember, I designed these questions without any consultation with them.

JUDGE SEYRANIAN: *Okay.*

DR. MALONY: I did not want, by any stretch of the imagination, the people I was talking to to know the questions in advance. So I might have phrased that a little differently.

What we were trying to get at was: Are there indiscriminate elders' meetings to which people are called on any regular basis and given the third degree?

JUDGE SEYRANIAN: *Oh! Okay. If you kind of had that as part of your oral questioning of these people, I can understand that. But if it is just as it's written here, I would hope, as you say, that the church does counsel them about their behavior. I think that's the purpose and the role of the church.*

DR. MALONY: That's right.

JUDGE SEYRANIAN: *And for the people to say, "No," I'm having difficulty understanding that. Would this be chance variation on question number seven, about being counseled?*

DR. MALONY: Yes, I guess. But let's remember that the book here makes an explicit statement or two: "We consider our reporting of these incidents typical of the practice of the 'Local Church.'" It does, I think, make that statement, does it not?

JUDGE SEYRANIAN: *Yes.*

DR. MALONY: And I am saying that you may have a chance variation. You see, in one of the depositions, I believe, by one of the expert witnesses, he reports a humiliation from one of his friends that led to becoming anxious or something. Well, that sounds like a chance variation, you know.

MR. MORGAN: *In other words, it doesn't reflect what is the practice?*

DR. MALONY: Not the typical practice. Now if I might give an example. Last year's superintendent of the Sunday school in my local church just left in a huff because she was not reappointed. The pastor did not go to see her. Now if somebody took that one incident and said that's typical of the practice of my church, I would say, "No."

JUDGE SEYRANIAN: *I think what you are telling me here is that what this question is in reference to is that the emphasis has to be "Counseled your behavior," meaning a one-on-one type thing.*

DR. MALONY: Yes.

JUDGE SEYRANIAN: *Rather than maybe in one of the lectures or something where they discuss each other's behavior, you are talking about a one-on-one situation?*

DR. MALONY: A calling in.

JUDGE SEYRANIAN: *A calling in?*

DR. MALONY: A calling in, yes.

MR. MORGAN: *And that's relating to authoritarianism and control, is it not?*

DR. MALONY: Yes. The picture that is painted in this book is that that is the practice; the elders spend their time that way, humiliating people.

JUDGE SEYRANIAN: *Did the people answering these questions understand that question as you have explained it to me now?*

DR. MALONY: I know what you are getting at; yes and no. I think that the very phrasing of my question may not have always drawn that out, but I would consider that would come out in their answers to this question. In some cases they would say, "What do you mean?" and I elaborated.

JUDGE SEYRANIAN: *Okay. All right.*

MR. MORGAN: *Do you also find, Doctor, that to some extent, eight and nine would qualify seven? In other words, what you are looking for here is the real authoritarian control?*

DR. MALONY: Yes. Yes.

MR. MORGAN: *All right. Now let me ask some basic conclusions now, or opinions, of yourself. First, have you formed an opinion whether the teachings of Witness Lee and the "Local*

Church" come within what is generally known as orthodox Christian teachings?

DR. MALONY: I have formed an opinion.

MR. MORGAN: *What is your opinion in that regard?*

DR. MALONY: I will say yes, they do, and I would qualify my statements.

MR. MORGAN: *By all means.*

DR. MALONY: Although I have a divinity degree and doctoral minor in contemporary theology, I do not want to present myself as a theological expert.

MR. MORGAN: *Okay. No problem.*

DR. MALONY: Okay.

MR. MORGAN: *I can put your mind at ease, because we had theologians on the other day.*

DR. MALONY: Okay.

MR. MORGAN: *Have you formed any opinion whether there was any mind manipulating by Witness Lee or the leaders of the "Local Church" through their teachings or their practices?*

DR. MALONY: Yes, I have formed an opinion.

MR. MORGAN: *What is your opinion?*

DR. MALONY: That there was none. I am equating the phrase "mind manipulating" with thought control, with brainwashing.

MR. MORGAN: *All right. Fine.*

DR. MALONY: There was social influence.

MR. MORGAN: *As opposed to if Witness Lee is teaching the Bible, and he is encouraging people to live a higher life than the Ten Commandments? That is some form of teaching, is it not?*

DR. MALONY: Of teaching, yes.

MR. MORGAN: *So hopefully it will have some effect on the mind of the individual?*

DR. MALONY: Indeed.

MR. MORGAN: *All right.*

DR. MALONY: As part of my data gathering, I contacted one of the prime experts in the Department of Defense, Major Robert Dussert, who has had no prior connection with the "Local Church" as far as I know. I submitted to him some materials, and we then dialogued. I reached a conclusion, he reached a conclusion, and we tried to compare notes. And as he said, "I see the practices as part of education or teaching or social influence. The practices of this church do not meet the criteria of brainwashing as understood in the literature and by the Department of Defense." And that's the same conclusion I reached in regards to brainwashing, mind control, or thought reform.

MR. MORGAN: *All right. Have you formed any opinion as to whether, either in the teachings or the practices, there is some threat or coercion to keep the members in the church?*

DR. MALONY: Generally, yes.

MR. MORGAN: *What is that opinion?*

DR. MALONY: That there is no threat or coercion.

MR. MORGAN: *All right.*

DR. MALONY: There is encouragement.

MR. MORGAN: *Have you formed any opinion as to whether there has been any psychological damage or whether there even should be any psychological damage on a member because of either the teachings or the practices of the "Local Church"?*

DR. MALONY: Yes.

MR. MORGAN: *What is your opinion?*

DR. MALONY: My opinion is that there is no evidence to that effect.

MR. MORGAN: *Have you formed any opinion that either in the teachings or the practices that there is some form of encouragement of engaging in immoral acts and justifying it because "inside of me it says okay"?*

DR. MALONY: Yes, I have formed an opinion.

MR. MORGAN: *What is your opinion?*

DR. MALONY: I find no evidence for that. Strong evidence the other way.

MR. MORGAN: *All right. In the talking to the ex-members of the "Local Church" and in reading the depositions of Mr. Smith and Mr. Painter, did you form any opinion that there was some loss of mental acuity by people once they left the "Local Church"?*

DR. MALONY: I have formed an opinion.

MR. MORGAN: *What is your opinion in that regard?*

DR. MALONY: On the basis of my talking with ex-members, I saw absolutely no evidence for that. They are all fully functioning human beings.

DR. MALONY: *Let's just talk another moment about your study. Do you feel that study is a fair representation of the responses of both ex- and present members of the church in regard to those questions?*

DR. MALONY: Let me say yes to that and then qualify it.

MR. MORGAN: *By all means.*

DR. MALONY: It is a much fairer representation than the data on which this book was written. From an ideal point of view, and this almost never happens in social science research, it would be nice to have random samples of ex-members and a larger number of surveys, but more times than not, we are content in this kind of research with this level of data, with what are called volunteer samples.

MR. MORGAN: *Okay. Speaking about the manuscript, Exhibit 1, what is it about their methodology, if there is such, that you feel your approach was fairer?*

DR. MALONY: They made no attempt, as far as I can tell, other than in an adversarial role, to do any interviewing of the experience of present members. They based all of their inferences, in the one case, on the report of one man, and at least they are honest enough to say that, one man who left under great turmoil and who spoke only after he left.

And in the other cases of ex-members, I don't believe they are named here, there is an amorphous ex-member group. I think you would find that ex-member reports, particularly of persons who left under duress, are all characterized in many groups by a hostility toward the group.

MR. MORGAN: *And does that hostility, then, in some way alter or temper the truth?*

DR. MALONY: Oh, I think it does. I don't want to use the word distortion, but it is a perceptual alteration. Let me hasten to add, Judge, that I'm not sure we know what social reality is. Every one of us sees through certain eyes. And members who are happy in a group are going to see that group more positively than those that are unhappy. And the truth is the other way, too.

MR. MORGAN: *Let me ask you this, do you believe that the results you got from your study fairly reflect and are consistent with what you observed at the church?*

DR. MALONY: Very consistent, yes. Very consistent.

MR. MORGAN: *Now let me ask you, in this appendix that you have referred to, could you class that as a psychological study?*

DR. MALONY: No.

MR. MORGAN: *And does it show any psychological scholarship or use of psychological methodology?*

DR. MALONY: It refers again and again to the writings or testimonies of certain psychologists and certain persons or groups that have written about social groups. My sense is that it is an essay written from a point of view using those resources in a truncated and, I would say, inappropriate manner.

MR. MORGAN: *Let me ask you, finally, do you have an opinion based upon your study (what you have been told and what you have read) as to what impact, if any, the charges that have been made and the books that have been published would have on Witness Lee and the "Local Church"?*

DR. MALONY: Yes.

MR. MORGAN: *Can you give us what that opinion is?*

DR. MALONY: It would be a negative impact.

MR. MORGAN: *And why?*

DR. MALONY: Because it would be guilt by association and guilt by innuendo of portraying Witness Lee as an authoritarian, cult-type leader, and the "Local Church" as a cult-type organization, both of which should be avoided.

MR. MORGAN: *Do you have any opinion as to the duration of this kind of damage on Witness Lee and this group? In other words, is this something that's transitory?*

DR. MALONY: The studies that have been done on rumor since the time of the Second World War suggest that rumor is very, very hard to counteract. It is best counteracted by the accusers, or those who start the rumor, correcting it. That's ideal. But when that doesn't occur, you are fighting an uphill battle often.

MR. MORGAN: *I once had a society editor testify in a libel case that gossip never dies. Would it be the same in rumor?*

DR. MALONY: I think it's similar because most people will say, "Where there is smoke, there is fire." There is some truth there, you see.

MR. MORGAN: *Thank you. I have no further questions.*

JUDGE SEYRANIAN: *We have had testimony here, Professor, that the days of McCarthyism, where you label somebody as a communist, even if you have a judicial trial that determines you are not a communist, it is a stigma that stays with you.*

Do you feel that if a certain group were classified as a cult in this day and age as the average layperson understands a cult, that stigma would remain in spite of the fact that, let's say, you had a judicial determination that it really is not a cult? Do you think some people still want to believe the worst in things until, as you say, the accusers retract, as they say?

DR. MALONY: I would presume so. Though I think the judicial process certainly would help in that regard. It's a little like the church-state issue, though. There are people who will say, "What does the state know about what we really know? How can they make a judgment in that case?" I think the judicial process is a very appropriate process because a group certainly has the right, being innocent, to be proven guilty and to confront their accusers.

I was interested in a recent Christian publication in which one of the advisers to the Spiritual Counterfeits Project, a social scientist like myself, made what I thought was an outlandish, naive statement, that in our day and age Christians can't accuse others of their heterodoxy, or something to that effect, without a fear of being sued. My thought was, we certainly have the right of free speech, but we have the responsibility of responsible speech of someone asking us what we mean, and if it is defamatory, I think there is a legal process that has the right to be undertaken, and certainly that does right the wrong at one level.

JUDGE SEYRANIAN: *What I am trying to get from you,*

because I think you probably have been the witness with the most studies in psychology and perhaps psychiatry–is there something about people that they always like to look for the worst in things, or is that an old farce that we hear that is really not true?

DR. MALONY: I think there is a segment in the Christian community, perhaps that segment having some of their own historical issues tied up in here, that does express their faith by confrontation and accusation. I don't think that mindset characterizes people in general or Christians in general.

JUDGE SEYRANIAN: *Okay.*

MR. MORGAN: *Can I ask one? But, Doctor, I think you know what the court is asking you. Let's assume that the court rules in favor of the plaintiffs here and, in effect, says, this is all false. Do you think that the stigma will, therefore, immediately evaporate—*

JUDGE SEYRANIAN: *Disappear.*

MR. MORGAN: —a*nd be gone forever?*

DR. MALONY: No. But I think that will have to be publicized. I think that will have to be believed.

MR. MORGAN: *Even then, do you think that will end it, or do you think there will still be those who feel that, well, they didn't know what they were doing or it was uncontested, or whatever else?*

DR. MALONY: I do think there will be some people who will feel the court didn't get all the facts or that the court has no business in it.

JUDGE SEYRANIAN: *Thank you very much.*

Chapter Seven

THE TESTIMONY OF
EDWIN S. GAUSTAD, Ph.D.

EDITOR'S NOTE: *Dr. Gaustad did not testify at the trial of* Lee vs. Duddy. *He did, however, research Witness Lee and the "Local Churches." The following is a paper he wrote as the conclusion of that study and updated last year in preparation for this book.*
Dr. Gaustad is Emeritus Professor of History at U.C. Riverside with a special interest in the history of American religion. He earned his Masters and Ph.D. in the History of Religion at Brown University (1948, 1951). A past president of the American Society of Church History, Dr. Gaustad is a foremost authority and author on the subject of American religions.

The courts in America have long recognized that the widest possible latitude is to be given to the free exercise of religion. A recent exception to that "long recognition," *Oregon Employment Division v. Smith* (1990), aroused so much criticism and anxiety that Congress in 1993 responded with a Religious Freedom Restoration Act that was signed into law that same year by President William Jefferson Clinton. By the enactment of this law, religious liberty was restored to its privileged position where only the most compelling state interest could justify any infringement upon its full and free exercise. It is the only freedom in the Bill of Rights to have a double guarantee: no favoritism on behalf of religion, no prohibition against religion. But as Thomas Jefferson observed in 1816, even if we have laws that provide for religious liberty, they lose much of their effectiveness if "we are yet under the inquisition of public opinion." When efforts are made to marshal public opinion against any religious group, but especially against one that is unfamiliar and politically powerless, then "free exercise" becomes a mockery. If in that effort to arouse public passion, statements are made which are malicious, inflammatory and even libelous, then the chilling effect upon religious liberty is compounded. Thus, the excess in the exercise of one freedom (of the press) severely limits or even destroys another freedom (of religion).

After the 1978 horror and tragedy of Jonestown in Guyana, the moment seemed especially ripe for self-appointed vigilante groups to denounce all non-traditional religious movements, to speak of "cults" and mental manipulation, of authoritarian figures and a religiously imposed isolation from the mainstream. Something sinister was suggested; something un-American or un-Christian must be going on in any group that did not fall under the familiar and "safe" labels of Methodist or Lutheran, Roman Catholic or Presbyterian. The late 1970s and early 1980s seemed the right time, the propitious time to "finish off" those vulnerable bodies that did not conform or were not in every way "orthodox" by someone's remarkably assured canon of truth. Such Spiritual Enforcers or Grand Inquisitors would, if successful, stifle all religious experimentation and smother all novel expression of the religious spirit. This is why it is necessary to challenge those who would ferret out and intimidate all who fail to "measure up" to some private standard of orthodoxy. To label those with whom one disagrees as nothing other than "Spiritual Counterfeits" who are to be defamed and denounced is to deny their First Amendment freedom of religion, even as it is to threaten the pluralistic nature of American society.

Fortunately, the courts in this land long ago abandoned the attempt to decide on orthodoxy or to punish heresy. As the U.S. Supreme Court observed in 1876 (Watson v. Jones), "the law knows no heresy." The court of public opinion, however, is not always so restrained. That opinion, aroused by unfair published attacks, can render a verdict more powerful and damaging than that given by any court of law.

It was under these circumstances that I was requested to examine the Local Church and evaluate the criticisms levied against it by the Spiritual Counterfeits Project and Neil Duddy. What can be said, then, about the Local Church and the Christian tradition in which it stands? Its detractors charge that the Local Church is on the one hand too authoritarian and that on the other it does not enforce sufficient discipline. What can this possibly mean? "Enforcers" complain that the Local Church teaches that Christians should not be tied to an external law, while ignoring their plain teaching to the contrary as well as the clear emphasis which the New Testament places upon the internal "fruits of the Spirit." Members of the Local Church, it is said, feel superior to all other religious groups and even speak contemptuously of them. The history of Christianity is replete with examples of those groups who, especially in their early years, manifest a zealous assurance and unique strength that seems strikingly different from the casual or inherited religious affiliation all around them. To persecute this zeal is to rob Christianity of the reforming impetus that it has always required. The Local Church is charged with placing greatest emphasis on the group. In this regard one might reflect upon the nature of every monastic community, every segregated and persecuted sect, every utopian colony from the Quakers to the Mennonites. These latter groups today find wide social acceptance even though their stress on community far exceeded that of the Local Church.

The most powerful conformity demanded in the nation today is probably cultural (gray flannel suits and all that). Ironically, the Local Church is simultaneously charged with rescuing its members from such a conformist society and at the same time with destroying their individuality! What the critics call "mental reformation," the proponents call conversion; the critics speak of abduction, the proponents of evangelization; the critics write in shock of "even alert, intelligent citizens" being "isolated from the social sphere in which they live and work"; proponents call it allegiance to God. The New Testament says nothing against reading newspapers or watching television; therefore, the Local Church by downplaying their importance is going beyond the New Testament—which, of course, also says nothing about shooting heroin, driving while drunk, or carrying concealed weapons. It is difficult to leave the Local Church, the

"Inquisitors" maintain, without suffering "severe insecurity" and psychic pain. So it is also, should one choose to leave Orthodox Judaism, Roman Catholicism, Greek Orthodoxy, Missouri Synod Lutheranism, or the Southern Baptist Convention. Even the Mennonites have problems with "shunning." Are all these groups, then, menacing cults, or spiritual counterfeits, or psychic threats?

Those who denounce the Local Church speak with such confidence of teachings or practices "that are totally alien to biblical Christianity." Blessed assurance these denouncers must have. For fifteen hundred years and more, sincere Christians have earnestly disagreed on the precise nature of "biblical Christianity." There is very little evidence in America or anywhere else in the world that universal agreement on this point is just around the corner.

In spite of an acknowledged diversity of opinion on "biblical Christianity," one wonders what the Spiritual Counterfeits Project had in mind in making so extreme a charge that the Local Church's teachings are "totally alien" to a Christian understanding drawn from biblical teaching. As one who has specialized in the study of Christianity in America, I cannot find valid ground for such an attack. The beliefs and practices of the Local Church constitute one more variation of emphases and themes familiar in Christian history. From my observation, I conclude that the Local Church stands in the tradition of evangelical Christianity, of the Protestant emphasis on biblical authority, of the great Christian mystics' and pietists' concern for the inner life, of the millennia-old expectation of a New Age, and of born-again, experiential religion. They meet together, pray together, sing and study together, and grow together. They labor to be loyal to their particular vision of the Christian life. It seems enough. It also sounds very much like the free exercise of religion.

RETRACTION REGARDING WITNESS LEE AND THE LOCAL CHURCHES

In 1977 *The Mindbenders,* a book authored by Jack Sparks, published by Thomas Nelson, Inc., accused Witness Lee and The Local Churches of being a cult and of being heretical in their beliefs. Both before and after publication of their first edition, Nelson received many letters from The Local Churches and their members protesting the falsity of the chapter concerning them. Notwithstanding these letters, Nelson published an expanded second edition in 1979. In 1980 Local Churches brought suit against Thomas Nelson and the author for libel. The Local Churches should not have been included in either edition of *The Mindbenders.* Nelson has no desire to inflict any damage or harm upon Witness Lee, The Local Churches, or their members by the continued publication of this book. Therefore, Nelson hereby retracts the statements made in *The Mindbenders* about them, and extends its apology to the good Christian members of The Local Churches. Accordingly, Nelson has withdrawn the book from publication and distribution and encourages all book sellers who have any unsold copies to return them for credit.

April 10, 1983   THOMAS NELSON, INC.

This retraction by Thomas Nelson, Inc. was published on Sunday, April 10, 1983 in the following newspapers:

Los Angeles Times
Dallas Morning News
Atlanta Journal/Constitution
Cleveland Plain Dealer
Chicago Tribune
New York Times
San Francisco Examiner & Chronicle
Washington Post
Wall Street Journal (Monday, April 11)

Akron Beacon Journal
Columbus Dispatch
Miami Herald
Raleigh News & Observer
Boston Globe
Orange County (Calif.) Register
Houston Chronicle
Oklahoma City Sunday Oklahoman
Seattle Times

INDEX

Throughout this index the abbreviation *GM* will be used to indicate references to *The God-Men,* lc to indicate the local church, SCP to indicate Spiritual Counterfeits Project, and WL to indicate Witness Lee. Dates or descriptions have been supplied in parenthesis after many names to aid the reader.

A

accusations of *GM*
  beliefs and practices 153
  no Christians outside lc 183
  religious and civil 94
  See also authoritarian accusations; moral accusations; psychological accusations; theological accusations
action research 168
adolescent religion 156
Alexander, Brooks (author, *GM I*) 104
allegiance to God, not isolation 199
altering consciousness 35, 119
Amen 121, 127, 176, 180
American Academy of Religion 21
American Board of Professional Psychologists 149
American Society of Church History 197
American Sociological Review 134
Anglican Church 110
Anselm (1033-1109) 116
anthropology of religion 87, 92, 102
anti-cult materials
  blindly accept and repeat *GM* 80
  development 41
  in Christian bookstores 32
  targets 42-43
  traced to Berkeley incident 52
anti-cult movement
  Christian 42
  secular 33, 38, 41
anti-nomian, without the law 69
apologists, Christian 23, 33
apology for *The Mindbenders* 14, 201
appeal to Caesar, lawsuit 13
Association for the Sociology of Religion 130

Athanasius the Great (295-373)
  "God became man so that we might become divine" 116
  mingling of God with man 125
Augustine, Bishop of Hippo (354-430)
  "love and do whatever you want" 100
Austin-Sparks, Theodore (1888-1971) 27
authoritarian accusations of *GM*
  authoritarian figure 46
  downgrading Scripture 59
  elders humiliate people 189
  hierarchy 31
  no discipline in church 73
  WL controls people's lives 165
  WL rules like a despot 101
  WL rules with an iron rod 45
authority of WL
  earned by labor over years 45
  respected leader 182
  upholding apostle Paul's authority 49
award, the testimony of this book 16

B

Babylon, interpreted to be Rome 107
Bainbridge, William (sociologist) 134
bankruptcy of SCP 14, 144
Baptists 200
Barker, Eileen (sociologist) 132, 138
Barth, Karl (1886-1968) Christ versus religion 54, 95
behavior, counseled about 173, 188
Berkeley Christian Coalition 22
Berkeley confrontations 51
Bible study 181
Bible, WL's view
  authority is absolute and unique 39

204 INDEX

Bible, WL's view *(continued)*
  authority is basis for experience 72
  basis for teaching 113
  complete divine revelation 67
  conservative interpretation 122
  die for 60, 61, 67, 113
  entire life spent teaching 67
  integral to experience 66
  live it 72
  not secondary 48, 58
  Old and New Testament 57
  study and learn 58
Bill of Rights 197
Birmingham Southern College 147
Book of Mormon 39
bookstores
  accept Watchman Nee 25, 81
  Christian 32, 41
  lc outlet in Chicago 27
  won't carry lc responses 13, 81
books quoted, by WL
  Christ and the Church Revealed and Typified in the Psalms 62
  Christ vs. Religion 54, 60, 99
  The Economy of God 68, 99
  How to Meet 47
  The Knowledge of Life 101
books, GM source for other writers 79
born-again, experiential religion 200
Boston Theological Institute 109
brainwashing 38-40, 76, 152, 182, 191
Brethren 22, 25, 27, 181
Bromiley, Professor G. D. (Fuller Seminary) 125
Brown University 197
Buddhism 24

C

calling on the Lord's name
  not brainwashing 105
  communal and vocal 36
Campolo, Dr. Anthony (Christian sociologist) 133
Catholic Church 109
  discourages immoral TV 187
  ex-members 200
  experiential dimension 178
  Jesuit order 86
  mass 93, 178
  pope not dictator 101
  uncomplimentary interpretation 107
  WL doesn't hate Catholics 107
Catholic priest 85, 95, 173

Catholic University 86
chance variation 170, 173, 175, 181, 188
charges, *See* accusations of *GM*
Children of God 38, 42, 117
children in lc
  behavioral observations 118-123
  treatment 92
Christ, personal relationship with 99
Christian Scientists 39
Christian World Liberation Front 22, 51, 87
Christianity
  built-up accretions 95
  mainline in America 22
Christianity Today 144
Christians outside the lc 183
church, one in each city 26, 126, 184
Clinton, Pres. William Jefferson 197
coercion, no sign of 78, 191
college campuses
  Christian apologists 23
  trouble evangelizing 80, 82
commentary by WL
  Genesis 113
  Exodus 113
  Psalms 62
  Romans 113
  First Corinthians 113
  Ephesians 113
  Revelation 107
commitment, not damaging 102
communism, stigma 52, 194-195
Congregationalist 25, 69
Constantine the Great (285-337) 163
contemplative order 35
contradictions of *GM* 72, 199
conversion
  not mental reformation 199
  theory of 131
counseled 103, 173, 188
cover of *GM* 106, 116-117
cross-examine, complete opportunity 15
cult definition, since 1930s
  doctrinal variation 37
  group you don't like 33
  marginal religious group 91
  non-biblical authorities 43
  non-Christian 33, 37, 41
  on the basis of beliefs 162
  sociological term 90
cult definition, since 1970s
  abandonment of families 123
  beyond doctrinal teaching 41
  brainwashing members 38

cult definition, since 1970s *(continued)*
   centralized authority 164
   children poorly treated 92
   deceitful recruiting 38
   deprogramming 41
   derogatory term 118, 141
   destructive, actively 33
   manipulating for devious ends 164
   Manson, Charles and Jim Jones 33
   pervasive cultural image 41
   psychological issues 38
   publicity, Jim Jones 41, 141
   religious lunatic fringe 123
   seduction toward evil end 91, 151
   undermine American values 32
cult groups
   Christian response to 88
   claiming Christian connection 42
   no Christian connection 43
   since 1930s 38, 39
   since 1970s 38, 41, 151
   study of 87
cults, parents afraid of 75, 115, 143

D

Darby, John Nelson (1800-1882) 22, 181
Decision, Statement of 15
default hearing 15
deliberate distortion
   careful misrepresentation of WL 113
   conclusion of experts 14
   Duddy did not misread Lee 50
   not accidental 94, 100
   quoting diametrically opposed 142
   reckless disregard of WL's words 73
   teaching of WL 69
   See also quotations out of context
Department of Defense 190
depositions 13-14, 93, 152
deprogramming 41, 76, 124
devil, eastern religion linked to 90
diabolical assertions 136
diagram altered 64
Diatribes of SCP 92
dictionary, only Christ 99
Disciples of Christ 184
disgruntled, *See* ex-members
dispensationalism
   law, ignore greater part 56
   Lee's theology 34
   revelation has been added 65
distortion, *See* deliberate
Doctrine and Covenants 39

Duddy, Neil T. (1950-1987)
   altered diagram 64
   claimed to research WL and lc 34
   completely misunderstood WL 29
   contradicts himself 72, 199
   deposition showed sophistication 50
   extraordinarily careless attacks 142
   GM, his book 15, 28
   invents sociological terms 133
   invents theological terms 97
   paper worthy of flunking 131
   robbed reforming impetus 198
   seminary degree 50, 156
   statements, false 43
   use of unconfirmed rumor 98, 142
   See also deliberate distortion; *GM*
Dussert, Major Robert (expert, brainwashing) 190

E

Eastern Orthodoxy 35, 119
eastern religions 35, 89
Edwards, Jonathan (1703-1758) 71
effect from *GM*
   average reader misled 68, 79
   cannot survive money charge 79
   creates cult image 11, 32, 117, 193
   cut off lc 30, 50, 51, 95, 99, 193
   impossible to counter charges 75
   isolate lc from society 95
   See also evangelicals, effect from *GM;* family fear caused by *GM;* gospel, effect from *GM*; reputation, effect from *GM*
elders' leadership 43, 101
Eliade, Mircea (historian of religions) 86
ellipses, misuse of 47
encouragement in lc
   glorify God, versus TV 159
   spend time learning the Lord 172
   spend time with the Bible and Christ 186
Encyclopedia of American Religions 20
Enroth, Ronald (SCP author) 90
Episcopal Church 124
Episcopal Divinity School 109
Episcopalians 112, 121
erasing cult image
   "like opening up a pillow to the wind and trying to recover the feathers" 32
   "not in my lifetime" 104
   very difficult 32, 104
   "won't immediately evaporate" 195
   See also effect from *GM*; stigma

INDEX

est 104
evangelical
  dispensational theology 56
  material 27
  movement 22
Evangelical Orthodox Church 22
evangelicals
  attack cults over doctrine 39
  forty million in U.S. 52
  gain converts 42
  Protestant Reformation, source 42
  pushed aside Christian brethren 52
  reject eastern discipline 35
evangelicals, effect from *GM*
  anathema 54, 115
  books take different position 50
  branded lc heretical 80
  devastating 144
  evangelicals defamed Christians 52
  misinformed 144
evangelization, not abduction 199
evidence, competent and reliable 15
ex-members in general
  adopt different world view 45
  biased view 89
  examples 89, 133, 200
  hostile toward group 192
  perceptual alteration 192
  shade the truth 45
ex-members of lc
  encouraged in lc to be ethical 174
  fully functioning human beings 192
  refused to sign affidavits 103
  testimony checked 14, 44
  See also survey questions
experience
  Bible integral to 66-72
  movements in Christian history 177-180

F

family fear caused by *GM*
  cults wafting away children 115
  members joining lc 75
fellowship in evangelical field 27
financial accusations of GM 79, 116, 142
Finney, Charles (1792-1875) 68-70
First Amendment 15, 198
footnotes, people don't check 51
free speech, yet responsibility 194
freedom of religion and press 198
Freeman, Willliam (plaintiff) 28, 43, 80, 131
Freud, Sigmund (1856-1939) 161

fruits and roots of religion 150
Fuller Theological Seminary 148
fundamentalism 22, 94

G

Garrett Theological Seminary 19
Gaustad, Edwin S. (expert, American religions) 9, 197-200
George Peabody College 147
gifts of the Spirit 48
glorify God, versus TV 159
goal of *GM*
  downgrade lc 94
  keep lc from getting converts 142-144
The God-Men (GM)
  contradicts itself 72
  Duddy's book 15, 28
  length of 34
  only book length study 80
  SCP's first big work 91
  source manuscript was same as *The Mindbenders* 12
  withdrawn from publication 16
  See also cover of *GM*; goal of *GM*; misrepresentation of *GM*; motive of *GM*; opinion of *GM*; title of *GM*
"God's frozen people" 112, 121
Goetchius, Eugene Van Ness (expert, theologian) 8, 109-127
gospel, effect from *GM*
  colleges, trouble evangelizing 80, 82
  outreach met complete rejection 13
  questions raised 83
Greek Orthodox 109, 200
growth of lc, steady to late 1970s 82
guru 35

H

Hari Krishnas 42, 117, 161, 180
Harvard Divinity School 124
Harvard University 109
Helter Skelter 139
heterodoxy
  Christians accusing of 194
  outside the Christian faith 163
Heythrop College 86
Hinduism, mantra 36
history of lc 26, 30
history of pray-reading
  German Pietists practiced 119
  missal and prayer book's purpose 119
  repetitious prayer is common 105

INDEX

history of pray-reading *(continued)*
  responsive reading 176
  See also observations of pray-reading;
    pray-reading
history of Watchman Nee 22-30
history of WL 22-26
Holiness people, sanctification 69
Holistic Health 24
honey, first taste of 71
hybrid, human-divine 62
hymnal of lc, doctrinally sound 118, 123
hyperbole 31, 58
hypnotism 179

I

idiocy 136
Ignatian Rule 179
imbibing the word 177
immorality discouraged 187, 191
inculcate Scripture 61
Independent Fundamentalis
  Churches 22
indigenous churches 26, 163
inspiration, divine and human 65
Institute for the Study of American
  Religion 19
Inter-Varsity Press 15, 143

J

James, William (psychologist) 150, 155
Jefferson, Thomas (1743-1826) 197
Jehovah's Witnesses 37, 40-42
Jesuit Theologate 109
Jesuits (Society of Jesus)
  comparison to lc 91, 96
  religious order 85
Jesus Christ, who is He? 185
Jesus People Movement 22
Jesus Prayer 105, 179
Jones, Jim
  authoritarian rule 45
  image of cult leader 41, 164
  juxtaposition to lc 117, 125
  ostracized people 74
Jonestown 13, 198
Journal for the Scientific Study of
  Religion 87, 149
Journal of American Scientific
  Affiliation 149
Journal of Ecumenical Studies 87, 89
Journal of Psychology and Christianity
  149

Journal of Psychology and Theology 149
Judaism 200
judicial determination 15-16, 194-195

K

Kinnear, Angus (author) 30

L

law, Old Testament
  church should have higher morality 115
  majority set aside 57-58
lawsuit
  appeal to Caesar 13
  forum to test the truth 13
  law knows no heresy 198
  not about theology 142
  results must be publicized 195
  why there was one 12
lay responsibility 44
Lee v. Duddy, et al 11
Lee, Witness (WL) *See* authority of
  WL; Bible, WL's view of; books
  quoted; commentary by WL; history
  of WL; opinion of WL; teaching of WL
libel 16, 142, 198
liberal Christians, modernists 60
Living Stream Ministry 28, 81
local church (lc)
  elders lead local congregations 43
  experts' awareness of 24, 110
  growth, steady until late seventies 82
  no hierarchy 44
  Plymouth Brethren category 22
  statement of faith 67
  See also children in lc; locality teaching;
    members of lc; name of lc; opinion
    of lc; opinion of lc members
locality teaching
  one church per city 26, 126, 184
  unity of Christendom 126
Lofland, John (sociologist) 132
Lofland-Stark model of conversion
  Duddy, diabolically the reverse 136
  misses the entire point 135, 155
  new religious belief system 134
  utilization by *GM* 134
  See also seduction syndrome
London School of Economics 132
Love Family in Seattle 139
love, 1 Cor. 13 67
Lutherans 200

M

Mahan, Asa (holiness leader) 68-70
Malony, H. Newton (expert, psychologist) 8, 147-195
Malta 86
Manson, Charles 41, 139
mantra
  comparisons to pray-reading 36, 105, 180
  See also pray-reading
Masons 151
McCarthyism, stigma 52, 194
meetings attended by experts
  "all-day affair" 76, 120
  devotional period 28
  in homes 28, 126
  lc 28, 75, 92, 112, 131
  pray-reading session 36, 153, 176
  WL lecture 122
  worship or training 152
meetings of lc
  "more lively than mass" 93
  not coerced participation 78
meetings with WL
  Goetchius 117
  Melton 28
  Saliba 98
Melton and Moore, *(The Cult Experience)* 156
Melton, John Gordon (expert, American religions) 7, 19-83, 117, 140, 145
members of lc
  age and conviction 184-185
  attitude and awareness of *GM* 77
  offended by *GM* 82
  See also opinion of lc members
Menninger Foundation 156
Mennonites
  group emphasis 199
  shun ex-members 200
metaphors describe experience 71
Methodists 78, 167
Methodist ideals of sanctification 69
Methodist minister 147
methodology of *GM* inadequate 166
The Mindbenders 12-14, 51, 81, 201
mind expansion 177
mingling 62, 81, 125
misrepresentation of *GM*
  altering diagram 62
  biblical authority and law 62
  Brethren affiliations 25, 30, 94
  Christian context of WL 93
  demonstrated in total 11
  Eastern religions 37

misrepresentation of *GM (continued)*
  ellipses, twisted use of 47
  history of lc 29, 94
  lc beliefs and practices 29, 31
  lc organization, from Brethren 31
  Lofland-Stark conversion model 138
  mingling, human-divine hybrid 62
  piety of lc 31
  pray-reading 31, 37
  simple answers to problems 157
  sociological trappings 132
  Benjamin Warfield's teaching 69
  WL's teaching 34, 93
  See also deliberate distortion
Modalism 185
modernists, liberal Christians 60
monastic tradition 35, 178, 199
Moon, Sun Myung 24
Moonies 42, 132, 138, 161, 163
moral pygmies 68, 69, 114, 125
moral accusations of *GM*
  below ethical code 68, 113, 142
  beyond human morality 116
  breaking moral law is okay 60
  conscience, none 68
  divine, so not bound by laws 61
  do what you want 97, 99
  encourage immorality 59, 60
  immoral and oblivious to fact 68, 72
  moral pygmies 68, 69, 114, 125
  not inculcated 95
  released from law 62
  See also accusations of *GM*
morality of lc
  immorality discouraged 187, 191
  righteousness exceeds Pharisees 114
  same as Saliba's 96
Mormonism 37, 39, 41, 42
motive of *GM*
  damage lc as much as possible 143
  exposed in depositions 15
  SCP second best 51
mouthpiece of God 46
"mystical oneness with God" 35

N

name of lc, given—not accepted 26
Nee, Watchman (1903-1972)
  bookstores accept writings 25, 81
  history 22-30
newspaper reading 158, 170-172, 187, 199
Nicene Creed 125
Northwestern University 19

INDEX

O

Oberlin Theological School 70
observations of pray-reading
  brainwashing, none 105
  experts' participation 36, 105, 176
  focused on Scriptures 176
  normal state of consciousness 36
  quite communal and vocal 36
  spontaneous 36, 176
  "time's up, let's have... coffee" 179
  See also pray-reading
Old Testament codification of law 56
one with the Lord in spirit 47
opinion of *GM*
  conclusions set at start 94, 141
  contradicts itself 199
  defamatory 151
  malicious 136
  name calling 94
  no sociological merit 131
  psychologists, improper use of 193
  relied on dissidents 44
  sloppy piece of scholarship 113
opinion of lc
  more enthusiastic 112
  found communion with 52
  nothing strange 93
  orthodox evangelical group 29, 141, 189, 200
  Plymouth Brethren, variety of 29
  related and could participate 92
  within conventional tradition 141
opinion of lc members
  above average intelligence 113, 122
  above conventional morality 125
  bright students 111
  enjoy their faith 77
  family-oriented 118
  good time at worship 78
  happy, not under bondage 77
  lives reveal *GM* is "absurd" 123
  moral integrity, no question 78
  not held against their will 77
  "square" 113
  understand and believe Bible 127
opinion of SCP literature
  doctrinal and psychological 38
  misunderstand groups studied 37, 103
  only write attacks 142
  summary criticism 89-92
opinion of WL
  biblically oriented 98
  encourages a higher life 190
  moral views, same 98

opinion of WL *(continued)*
  no problem fellowshipping with 29
  Protestant in spirit 98
oracle of God 46
orthodox, hold Christian basics 29

P

parents, afraid of cults 75, 115, 143
Pearl of Great Price 39
Pearls, Fritz (Gestalt psychologist) "get out of your mind and come to your senses" 178
pejorative terms 52, 68, 119, 141
People's Temple 125
pinko, labeling of 52
Plymouth, *See* Brethren
pray-reading
  deepens experience 177-178
  digests the word 119
  form of lc prayer 31, 140
  imbibing the word 177
  See also history of pray-reading; observations of pray-reading
Presbyterian teaching 100
Presbyterian sanctification 69
prophecy, most important gift 48
Protestant Reformation 42
protests made before publication 12
Psalms, some more spiritual 64
psychological accusations of *GM*
  altered consciousness 105, 175
  brainwashing 104
  damage, no sign 73, 191
  hospitalization 74
  hypnosis, told to do evil 181
  lose mental control 73, 175
  manipulation 43
  public humiliation 74
  zombies 104, 119, 181
  See also seduction syndrome
psychology of religion 148

Q

Quakers, group emphasis 199
quasi-divine 182
questions raised in new ones 83
quotations out of context 47, 61, 100, 107, 125

R

radio 158, 165, 170-172, 186-187

random sample, for survey 167
Rapoport, Max 74, 182
reading done by experts
  depositions 93, 152
  Duddy manuscript 28, 112
  Freeman books 28
  GM 31, 92, 93, 124
  WL books 28, 67, 74, 75, 112, 131, 152
references
  Beliefs and Practices of the Local Churches 125
  The Cult Experience 156
  The Experience of Life 125
  Galatians 125
  How to Meet 125
  Matthew 18:15 12
  The Normal Christian Life 25, 112, 122
  The Practical Expression of the Church 125
  Romans 125
  The Testimony of Church History Regarding the Mingling of God with Man 125
  The Vision of God's Building 125
  Who is the Real Mindbender? 81
  See also books quoted
religion, paraphrased definition 54
Religious Freedom Restoration Act 197
repetitious prayer examples 105, 178
reputation, effect from *GM*
  branded WL deceptive 80
  cut off lc 80
  damaged reputations 71, 98, 106
  guilt by association and innuendo 193
  like charging with witchcraft 75
  very difficult recovering 32
research done by experts
  member contact 76, 77, 131
  toured Living Stream 28
  videotapes 28, 74, 112, 131, 153
  See also meetings attended by experts; reading done by experts; observations of pray-reading
responses published 80
retraction of *The Mind Benders* 14, 201
Review of Religious Research 149
roots and fruits of religion 150
rumor
  Duddy did not check charges 98
  hard to counteract 193
  GM is worst kind 142
  lingers on though *GM* withdrawn 16
  people unfortunately believe 104
  "where there's smoke, there's fire" 194

S

Saliba, John Albert (expert, anthropology of religion) 7, 85-107
sanctification, in simple language 69
Science and Health 39
scissors-and-paste method 94
Scripture
  imbibe 177
  inculcate 61
Scripture quoted
  Psalm 121 176
  John 1:14 125
  John 14:20 125
  John 14:11, 23 116
  Romans 2:29 55
  Romans 7:6 55
  1 Corinthians 12-14 48
  1 Corinthians 13 61, 67
  2 Corinthians 3:18 55
  Ephesians 4:4 126
  1 Timothy 1:19, 20 74
  2 Timothy 3:16-17 60
  Revelation 17 107
secular anti-cult groups 38
seduction syndrome 133, 153-158
sensuous theology
  discount moral law 60
  experts couldn't find term 114
  honey, first taste of 71
  immorality attributed to 114
  invented 71
  stresses experience, not Scripture 71
Separatists
  claim to be the only church 184
  de-emphasis on worldly ways 159
  discourage television watching 171
  example groups cited 159-160
  sect church label 160
Seventh-day Adventists 40
Seyranian, Judge Leon 15
shunning common among groups 200
social anthropology 86
social conditioning 40
social influence 190
social science 132
Society of Biblical Literature 122
sociology of religion 130, 160
source for other books, *GM* is 79
Sparks, Jack (author of *The Mindbenders*, retracted by publisher) 12, 22, 27, 51, 81, 201
spirit, One with the Lord in 47
Spiritual Counterfeits Project (SCP)
  anti-cult organization 23, 32

INDEX 211

Spiritual Counterfeits Project *(continued)*
  evangelical group 42
  evangelicals' consumer research 144
  experts' awareness of 21, 87
  history 22
  not a formal religion 22
  number of writers, small 90
  self-proclaimed experts 11
  special task assigned 37, 142
  veto power by cult label 81
  See also opinion of SCP
spiritual director 35
Spiritualism 40
Squires, Ervin (SCP member) 103
Stark, Rodney (expert, sociologist) 8, 129-145
Stewart, Charles (psychologist) 156
stigma
  communism 52, 194-195
  McCarthyism 52, 194
  See also erasing cult image
Studiorum Novi Testamenti Societas 122
survey questions 165

T

Talmud 56
teaching of evangelicals
  Bible is unique authority 39, 42
  living Scripture is sign of belief 67
  never degrade Bible 53
  people of the Book 42
  Scripture inspired by God 66
  teaching of the living Christ 67
teaching of WL
  books, transcriptions of talks 34
  Christ versus religion 55
  Christian faith, concisely 112
  develop the mind 74
  dispensationalism 34
  do not pray for guidance against law 59, 68
  experiential emphasis 61, 71, 114
  faith, most important thing 66
  fundamentals 60
  inculcate Scripture in lives 61
  law is divine but superseded by Christ's revelation 66
  man cannot become part of Godhead 125
  must follow law's moral aspect 59, 96
  one church in each city 126
  Psalms, some more spiritual 64
  public and private, the same 34
  subordination of children 120

teaching of WL *(continued)*
  teacher-preacher with hyperbole 31, 58
  teaching of the living Christ 66
  written code versus Christ 56
  See also Bible, WL's view
television watching 97, 157, 161, 170-172, 186-187, 199
Temple University 87
Ten Commandments
  cannot be changed 68
  Christ's added dimension 96
  for all times, places, people 59
  immutable laws must be followed 57
Theological Studies 87
theological accusations of *GM*
  Bible discounted 46, 53, 65-67, 113
  distorted Bible study 181
  pagan rather than biblical 35
  public and private 34
  sensuous theology 60, 71
  spiritualized theology 59
  See also accusations of *GM*
Theosophy 40
Time magazine 117
title of *GM* 62, 115
Transcendental Meditation 89, 104, 161, 180
Trinity 32, 81, 185
truth, experts concerned about *GM* issue 52, 142

U

Unification Church 89, 117, 132
United States, a Christian nation 163
unity of Christendom 126
University of California at Berkeley 129
University of California at Riverside 197
University of California at Santa Barbara 20
University of Denver 129
University of Detroit 85
University of Oxford 86
University of Pennsylvania 133
University of San Francisco 85
University of Virginia 109
University of Washington 129, 134, 143

V

Vanderbilt University 147
videotapes, *See* research done
vigilante groups, self-appointed 198
volunteer samples of survey 192

W

Warfield, Benjamin (1851-1921) 69, 114
Wesley, John (1703-1791) 161, 182
Weston School of Theology 109, 124
Wilson, Woodrow, World War I 70
world-denying
  avoid temptations 160
  Christian community accepts 160
  See also Separatists
worldly ways, examples of 159, 172

Y

Yale Divinity School 147
Yoga 89

Z

zeal of lc 199
Zen 89
zombie, *See* pejorative terms;
  psychological accusations of *GM*